# Ready-to-Use

# SOCIAL SKILLS LESSONS & ACTIVITIES

## for Grades PreK-K

 **RUTH WELTMANN BEGUN, Editor**
The Society for Prevention of Violence
with
The Center for Applied Research in Education

A ready-to-use curriculum based on real-life situations to help you
build children's self-esteem, self-control, respect for the
rights of others, and a sense of responsibility for one's own actions.

THE CENTER FOR APPLIED
RESEARCH IN EDUCATION
West Nyack, New York 10994

**Library of Congress Cataloging-in-Publication Data**

Ready-to-use social skills lessons & activities for grades pre-K–K
    Ruth Weltmann Begun, editor.
        p.    cm. — (Social skills curriculum activities library)
    Includes bibliographical references.
    ISBN 0-87628-863-8
    1. Social skills—Study and teaching (preschool).    2. Education,
Preschool—Activity programs.    3. Behavior modification.    I. Begun,
Ruth Weltmann.    II. Series.
    LB1139.S6R43    1995                                                95-5194
    646.7′071—dc20                                                    CIP

Printed in the United States of America

10   9   8   7   6

ISBN 0-87628-863-8

**THE CENTER FOR APPLIED RESEARCH
IN EDUCATION**

West Nyack, NY 10994

On the World Wide Web at http://www.phdirect.com

# ABOUT THIS SOCIAL SKILLS TEACHING RESOURCE

Today's educators carry added responsibilities because significant social changes have had an impact on human relations. Family ties have been loosened. The number of single-parent families has grown. Stresses in many families are often high. Thus, youngsters are frequently exposed to influences which tend to make them aggressive and possibly violent. Moreover, television, now in almost every home, frequently shows events not suitable for guiding children. Youngsters who cannot read and write watch violent scenes and might draw wrong conclusions. Unless schools, daycare centers, head start programs, and parents counteract asocial influences starting at the pre-kindergarten level, verbal and physical interpersonal abuse and violence will be an increasing problem.

This resource is one of four books in the "Social Skills Curriculum Activities Library," a practical series designed to help teachers, care givers and parents in giving children regular social skills lessons. The full Library spans all grade levels, preschool through grade 12, and includes:

**READY-TO-USE SOCIAL SKILLS LESSONS & ACTIVITIES FOR GRADES PreK-K**
**READY-TO-USE SOCIAL SKILLS LESSONS & ACTIVITIES FOR GRADES 1-3**
**READY-TO-USE SOCIAL SKILLS LESSONS & ACTIVITIES FOR GRADES 4-6**
**READY-TO-USE SOCIAL SKILLS LESSONS & ACTIVITIES FOR GRADES 7-12**

Each grade-level book provides 50 or more detailed, age-appropriate lessons for developing specific social skills accompanied by reproducible activity sheets and other activities to help students learn the skill. The lessons are presented in a uniform format and follow a Structured Learning approach to teach the skills. They focus on real situations in children's own lives, such as dealing with feelings and peer pressure, and are readily adapted for use in any classroom, school, or home setting.

The lessons and activities in Books one, two, and three are followed by two special sections entitled "Social Skills Task Review" and "Social Skills Family Training Booklet." "Social Skills Task Review" presents 21 social skills topics that can be used for teacher-led discussions during Circle Time. These are printed in the form of discussion cards which can be photocopied and cut out for use at the appropriate time. You can introduce each topic once before studying a skill and later, following the lesson, to measure what children have learned. The Social Skills Family Training Booklet is addressed to parents and single pages can be copied as needed for use with individual children. The booklet includes a brief introduction to its purposes and acknowledgement to its originators followed by a family social skills checklist, and helpful hints and reminders for using the booklet and teaching social skills effectively. The heart of the booklet is comprised of "Fourteen Selected Social Skills" with suggested skill activities that can be done within the family.

NOTE: Copies of the booklet can be ordered from the publisher, The Center for Applied Research in Education, at the minimum quantity of 20.

Most of the lessons and activities in the Social Skills Library were written, edited, and classroom-tested by teachers from the Cleveland (Ohio) Public Schools in cooperation with faculty from John Carroll University's Department of Education. The project was funded by The Society for Prevention of Violence (SPV), a non-profit organization founded by S.J. Begun, Ph.D., and his wife Ruth Weltmann Begun, M.S., and sponsored by them and various contributing corporations and foundations. Many individual members of the SPV also made substantial contributions. Specific credits are given on the Acknowledgments page.

Major objectives of teaching these lessons are to build students' self-esteem, self-control, respect for the rights of others, and a sense of responsibility for one's own actions. Another objective is to teach the students to settle grievances and conflicts through communication without recourse to violence. We believe that such training can be effective and successful by increasing discipline and reducing the drop-out rate. Thus, students will benefit from social skills training throughout their lives.

*S.J. Begun, Ph.D.*

*Ruth Weltmann Begun, M.S.*

The Society for Prevention of Violence

THE SOCIAL SKILLS SONG
(Tune: "Mary Had a Little Lamb")

WE CAN USE OUR SOCIAL SKILLS
SOCIAL SKILLS, SOCIAL SKILLS
WE CAN USE OUR SOCIAL SKILLS
AS WE SPREAD OUR GOOD WILL

EVERY DAY IN EVERY WAY
EVERY WAY, EVERY WAY
EVERY DAY IN EVERY WAY
OUR CHARACTER WE BUILD

# ACKNOWLEDGMENTS

The Founders, Trustees, Members, Friends of the Society for Prevention of Violence (SPV), and many foundations and corporations sponsored the writing of the social skills training material in the "Social Skills Curriculum Activities Library" with the objectives of reducing interpersonal violence and solving controversies in an amicable way.

Credit for writing the PreK-K lessons and activities in Volume 1 in the Library belongs to a collective effort by a group of teachers and administrators of the Cleveland (Ohio) Public Schools who had unique experience in teaching pre-kindergarten and kindergarten children. They wrote under the direction of four professors from the Department of Education of the John Carroll University in Cleveland, Ohio, assisted by consultants of the Society for Prevention of Violence (SPV). The concept of a curriculum was initiated by the then Executive Director of SPV, Ruth Weltmann Begun, who did the final page collection and editing of the finished manuscripts for the Curriculum.

# ABOUT THE SOCIETY FOR PREVENTION OF VIOLENCE (SPV)

The Society for Prevention of Violence (SPV) is dedicated to reducing the prevalence of violent acts and asocial behaviors in children and adults through education. It accomplishes this mission by teaching children and adults the use of the skills necessary to build their character, helping them acquire a strong values system, motivating them to develop their communication skills and to realize growth in interpersonal relationships. The mission includes integration of social and academic skills to encourage those who use them to reach their full potential and contribute to our nation's society by being able to make decisions and solve problems through effective and appropriate means.

As a non-profit organization, the Society had its origin in 1972 as The Begun Institute for the Study of Violence and Aggression at John Carroll University (Cleveland, Ohio). A multitude of information was gathered, studied, and analyzed during the ensuing ten-year period. Symposia were held which involved numerous well-known presenters and participants from various career fields. Early on, the founders of the Institute, S.J. and Ruth Begun, foresaw the trend of increasing violence in our families, communities and across the nation, and chose to take a leadership role in pioneering an educational approach to help alleviate aggressive and antisocial behavior. The educational approach was and continues to be the sole PROACTIVE means to change behaviors. Current conditions reflect our society's reliance on reactive means of dealing with this problem. During the next ten-year period, through the determination and hard work of Ruth Weltmann Begun as executive director, the workshops, parent training sessions, collaborative projects, and a comprehensive (preschool through grade 12) Social Skills Training Curriculum were developed.

Today, classroom teachers in numerous school districts across the country are utilizing this internationally recognized curriculum. The Society continually seeks support through individual donors, grants, direct paid services, and material/consultant service sales. It also has expanded its involvement in the educational process by:

▶ publishing a semiannual newsletter and other pertinent articles;

▶ providing in-service training for professional staffs, parents, and others;

▶ providing assistance in resource identification, proposal writing/project design and evaluation;

▶ tailoring instructional (academic and other) delivery designs to specific school/organization needs; and

▶ implementing pilot demonstration projects with foundation support.

As we move into and through the twenty-first century, we must work diligently and cooperatively to turn challenges into success.

The Society also offers graduate-level workshops in cooperation with John Carroll University for educators. Credits earned in these workshops may be applied toward renewal of certificates through the Ohio Department of Education.

For further information, contact The Society for Prevention of Violence, 3439 West Brainard Road #102, Woodmere, Ohio 44122 (phone 216/591-1876) or 3109 Mayfield Road, Cleveland Heights, Ohio 44118 (phone 216/371-5545).

# ABOUT THE SOCIAL SKILLS CURRICULUM

## *Philosophy*

We believe that the learning of social skills is the foundation for social and academic adequacy. It assists in the prevention of social problems and leads to successful functioning and survival skills for our citizens. Social behavior and academic behavior are highly correlated. We believe it is more productive to teach children the proper ways to behave than to admonish them for improper behavior. This requires direct and systematic teaching, taking into consideration social and developmental theory in the affective, cognitive, and psycho-motor domains. Learning should be sequential, linked to community goals, and consistent with behaviors which are relevant to student needs. This social skills curriculum is based on these beliefs.

## *Curriculum Overview*

As children grow, one way they learn social behaviors is by watching and interacting with other people. Some children who have failed to learn appropriate behaviors have lacked opportunities to imitate good role models, have received insufficient or inappropriate reinforcement, or have misunderstood adequate social experiences.

The Social Skills Curriculum is designed to teach these behaviors in ways that correlate with child development theory, namely how children learn in their natural environment. Each lesson provides models for children to imitate and correction strategies following practice of the skills. The teacher and the rest of the class then provide positive reinforcement to encourage the continued use of the appropriate skills in situations that occur in any environment.

Teachers using this curriculum can be flexible. The curriculum is designed to be used in the classroom as lessons taught for about 20-30 minutes, two to three times a week. However, it is not the intent that these be the only times social skills are taught and learned. Every opportunity should be used to reinforce, model, and coach the children so that they can practice the skills enough to feel comfortable with them as part of their ways of behaving. Therefore, the teacher should remind the students of the skills and the need to use them in all appropriate situations once the skills have been demonstrated. The teacher should also plan to model the skills in any and all interactions with the children. The teacher should be *consistent* in not only using the skills when they are taught, but in using them in all interactions with the students. Only this kind of consistent modeling will assure that the children will see the skills used repeatedly and begin to know and feel comfortable with using them. Teachers should also feel free to adapt the material to class needs and to design and develop strategies, models, and interventions other than those suggested here. Students can even be involved in helping to think of modeling strategies and other techniques.

The Social Skills Curriculum Library is graded pre-Kindergarten through Grade Twelve and presented in four volumes focusing on four different levels: grades preK-K, 1-3, 4-6, and 7-12. It uses a structured learning approach to teach the skills. *Structured Learning* is a holistic teaching method that provides a framework for systematic teaching in a way that is similar to academics. The emphasis in this curriculum is to provide constructive and structured behaviors for socially skill-deficient children.

Structured Learning consists of *four basic components:* modeling, role playing, discussion of performance, and use in real-life situations. For more effective teaching, the lessons include eight steps that follow a directed lesson format (see below):

*Social Skill:* A social behavior that is directly observable.

*Behavioral Objective:* An expected outcome of learning the social skill that can be evaluated.

*Directed Lesson:* Each behavior is defined and stated in observable terms; the behavior is demonstrated and practiced; a student's level of performance is evaluated and inappropriate behaviors are corrected. Positive reinforcement is used to encourage continued use of the skill in all areas of the student's environment.

1.  *Establish the Need:* The purpose of teaching the lesson is included. What benefits will learning the skill provide? What are the consequences of not learning the behavior?

2.  *Introduction:* Stories, poems, puppets, and questions are used to make the social skill more concrete to the children.

3.  *Identify the Skill Components:* These skill steps are used to teach the behavior. By following and practicing these steps, the students will be able to demonstrate the behavior when needed.

4.  *Model the Skill:* The teacher or socially adept child demonstrates the appropriate behaviors so that the students can imitate them. The skill components are referred to during the modeling.

5.  *Behavioral Rehearsal:* The children are given an opportunity to perform the behavior which can be evaluated, corrected, and reinforced.

    A. *Selection*—The teacher selects participants or asks for volunteers. The number of children depends on the time allowed and whatever is appropriate for each lesson.

    B. *Role Play*—The participants are assigned their roles or situations they will role play.

    C. *Completion*—This is a means to determine that the role playing is complete. After each role play, reinforce correct behaviors, identify inappropriate behaviors, and reenact role play with corrections. If there are no corrections, role play is complete.

    D. *Reinforcers*—Positive reinforcement by the teacher and the class is used for maintenance of the skill. Various methods can be used: verbal encouragement, tangible rewards, special privileges, and keeping a record of social and academic improvement.

    E. *Discussion*—The student's level of performance is evaluated and inappropriate behaviors are corrected. How did the participants feel while performing? What difficulties might be faced in implementing the skill? What observations did the class make?

6.  *Practice:* Activities that help the children summarize the skill. The practice can be done by using worksheets, doing art projects, making film strips, writing stories, keeping diaries and charts, and so on.

7.  *Independent Use:* Activities that help facilitate the use of these behaviors outside the school environment. Family and friends take an active role in reinforcing the importance of using these alternative behaviors in a conflict situation.

8.  *Continuation:* At the end of each lesson, the teacher reminds the class that applying social skills can benefit them in academic and social relationships. Stress that, although there are difficulties in applying the skills (such as in regard to negative peer pressure), the benefits outweigh the problems. One such benefit is more self-confidence in decision-making. Maintaining social behavior is an ongoing process. It requires teachers to show appropriate behaviors and reinforce them when they are demonstrated.

# STRUCTURED LEARNING

## FOUR BASIC COMPONENTS

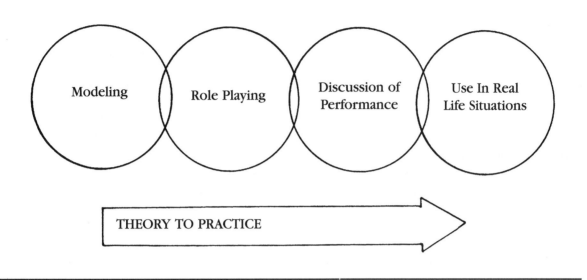

Modeling

Role Playing

Discussion of Performance

Use In Real Life Situations

THEORY TO PRACTICE

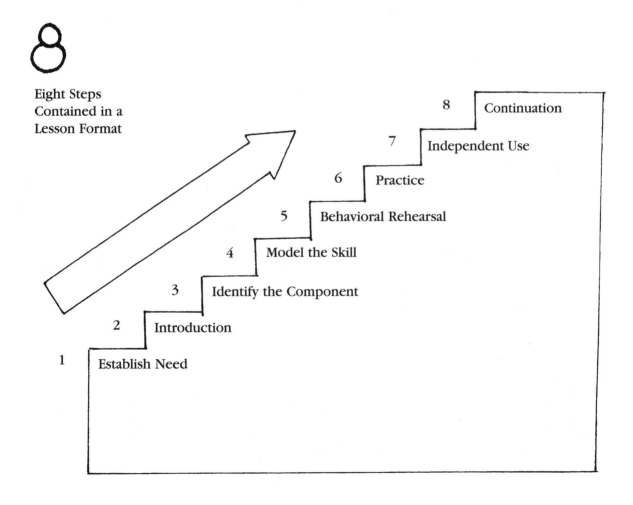

Eight Steps
Contained in a
Lesson Format

8 Continuation

7 Independent Use

6 Practice

5 Behavioral Rehearsal

4 Model the Skill

3 Identify the Component

2 Introduction

1 Establish Need

# BIBLIOGRAPHY

## Books

Apter, Stephen J., and Arnold P. Goldstein. *Youth Violence: Program and Prospects.* Needham Heights, MA: Allyn & Bacon, 1986.

Ballare, Antonia, and Angelique Lampros. *Behavior Smart! Ready-to-Use Activities for Building Personal and Social Skills for Grades K-4.* West Nyack, NY: Center for Applied Research in Education, 1994.

Cartledge, Gwendolyn, and Joanne Fellows Milburn. *Teaching Social Skills to Children,* 2nd ed. Needham Heights, MA: Allyn & Bacon, 1986.

Cherry, Clare. *Please Don't Sit on the Kids: Alternatives to Punitive Discipline.* Belmont, CA: Fearon-Pitman, 1982.

Chirinian, Helene. *Cartoon Comprehension.* Redondo Beach, CA: Frank Schaeffer Publications, 1980.

Eberle, Bob. *Help! in Managing Your Classroom.* Carthage, IL: Good Apple, 1984.

Farnette, C., I Forte, and B. Loss. *I've Got Me and I'm Glad*, rev. ed. Nashville, TN: Incentive Publications, 1989.

Feshbach, Norma, and Seymour Feshbach et al. *Learning to Care: Classroom Activities for Social and Affective Development.* Glenview, IL: Good Year Books, 1983.

Ginott, Haim G. *Teacher and Child: A Book for Parents.* New York: Macmillan, 1984.

Goldstein, Arnold P., Stephen J. Apter, and Berj Harootunian. *School Violence.* Englewood Cliffs, NJ: Prentice Hall, 1984.

Goldstein, Arnold P. et al. *Skillstreaming the Adolescent: A Structured Learning Approach to Teaching Prosocial Skills.* Champaign, IL: Research Press, 1980.

Grevious, Saundrah Clark. *Ready-to-Use Multicultural Activities for Primary Children.* West Nyack, NY: Center for Applied Research in Education, 1993.

Kaplan, P.G., S.K. Crawford, and S.L. Nelson. *Nice.* Denver: Love, 1977.

Mannix, Darlene. *Be a Better Student: Lessons and Worksheets for Teaching Behavior Management in Grades 4-9.* West Nyack, NY: The Center for Applied Research in Education, 1989.

____. *Life Skills Activities for Special Children.* West Nyack, NY: Center for Applied Research in Education, 1991.

____. *Social Skills Activities for Special Children.* West Nyack, NY: Center for Applied Research in Education, 1993.

McElmurry, Mary Ann. *Caring.* Carthage, IL: Good Apple, 1981.

____. *Feelings.* Carthage, IL: Good Apple, 1981.

McGinnis, Ellen, and Arnold P. Goldstein. *Skillstreaming the Elementary School Child: A Guide for Teaching Prosocial Skills.* Champaign, IL: Research Press, 1984.

Schwartz, Linda. *The Month-to-Month Me.* Santa Barbara, CA: The Learning Works, 1976.

Standish, Bob. *Connecting Rainbows.* Carthage, IL: Good Apple, 1982.

Stephens, Thomas M. *Social Skills in the Classroom,* 2nd ed. Lutz, FL: Psychological Assessment Resources, 1992.

Stull, Elizabeth Crosby. *Multicultural Discovery Activities for the Elementary Grades.* West Nyack, NY: Center for Applied Research in Education, 1994.

Teolis, Beth. *Ready-to-Use Self-Esteem Activities for Grades 4–8.* West Nyack, NY: Center for Applied Research in Education, 1995.

Toner, Patricia Rizzo. *Relationships and Communication Activities.* West Nyack, NY: Center for Applied Research in Education, 1993.

____. *Stress Management and Self-Esteem Activities.* West Nyack, NY: Center for Applied Research in Education, 1993.

## Documents

Early Identification of Classification of Juvenile Delinquents: Hearing Before the Subcommittee of the Committee on the Constitution, U.S. Senate, 97th Congress; Serial No. J-97-70; October 22, 1981; Testimony by: Gerald R. Patterson, Research Scientist—Oregon Social Learning Center, Eugene, Oregon; David Farrington, and John Monahan.

*Ounces of Prevention: Toward an Understanding of the Causes of Violence*; by State of California Commission on Crime Control and Violence Prevention, 1982.

# DEMONSTRATING WITH HAND PUPPETS

Puppets appeal to all ages, children and adults alike, and afford an excellent means to act out the situations, emotions, and skills portrayed in the social skills lessons in this book. Moreover, a hand-crafted puppet is much better than one bought in a store. It is truly one of a kind.

The following pages present a variety of reproducible patterns for making hand puppets for use with many of the lessons: "Sensitive Sam Hand Puppet" and "Social Sue Hand Puppet," clown hand puppets, and stick puppets. The patterns can be photocopied just as they appear and used to make:

(1) Stationary Puppets: Color, cut out, glue onto cardboard, and tape onto a stick handle.

(2) Movable Puppets: Color, cut out, and glue onto felt shapes. Insert the hand inside the felt shapes so that the puppets can move.

Of course there are many varieties of hand puppets, each having a character and personality of its own, and equally suitable for demonstrating the situations and skills in the lessons. Examples include finger puppets, box puppets, paper bag puppets, glove and mitten puppets, and cylinder or tube puppets. Easy-to-follow, illustrated directions for making each of these types of puppets and others may be found in *Let's Discover Puppets* (West Nyack, NY: The Center for Applied Research in Education), by Jenean Romberg.

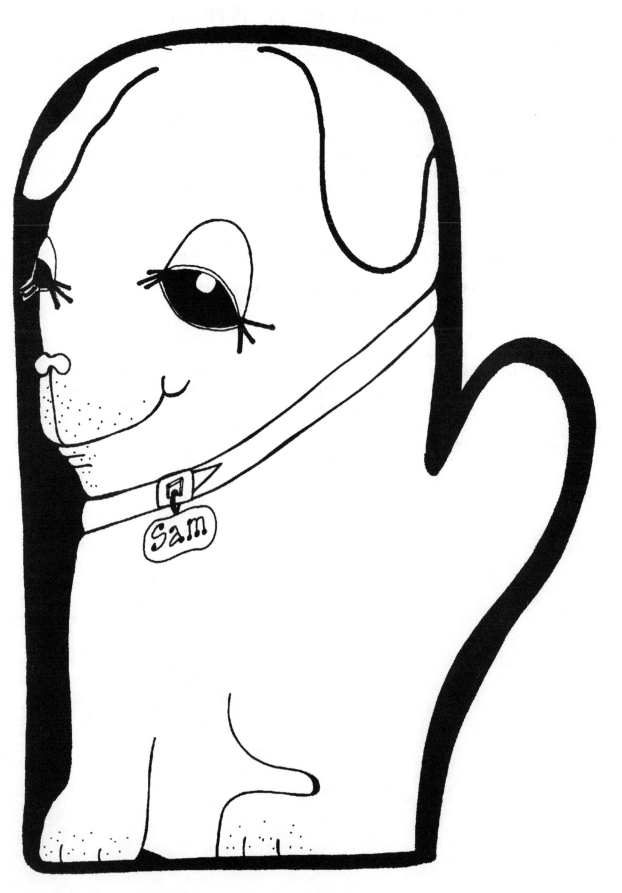

# CONTENTS

> *Reproducibles*    "Sensitive Sam" Hand Puppet
> "Social Sue" Hand Puppet
> Candy the Clown Hand Puppet
> Crackers the Clown Hand Puppet
> Morty Mouse Stick Puppet
> Maggie Mouse Stick Puppet

## SOCIAL SKILLS LESSONS & ACTIVITIES FOR GRADES PreK-K

*Asterisked lessons are especially appropriate for younger children.

*Contents*

Contents

## "PARTNERS IN SOCIAL SKILLS: A FAMILY AFFAIR"
### (SINGLE PAGES REPRODUCIBLE AS MARKED)

# SOCIAL SKILLS LESSONS & ACTIVITIES
## FOR GRADES PreK-K

# TO THE TEACHER

The following pages present 50 ready-to-use social skills lessons with a variety of related activities and worksheets. All of the lessons have been tested and are suggested for use with preschool and kindergarten (PreK-K) children. Lessons highlighted with an asterisk are particularly suitable for younger children.

The lessons may be used in any order you desire, though they are sequenced in a general way, beginning with disciplinary strategies for the classroom. Ultimately, of course, you will match the needs and ability levels of your pupils with the particular lessons and social skills learning objectives. Some of the lessons may have to be repeated several times over the course of the school year.

You may want to introduce a social skill in class discussion before presenting the related lesson, as suggested in the "Social Skills Task Review" on page 154. This should give you an idea of how familiar children may or may not be with the skill. The skill can then be discussed by the class again following the lesson to see how many children have learned this skill.

The patterns and worksheets accompanying these lessons may be photocopied as many times as you need them for use with individual children, small groups, or the whole class. You may also devise activity sheets of your own to enrich and reinforce any of the lessons.

## SOCIAL SKILL
### *Understanding the Need for Rules*

***Behavioral Objective:*** The children will need to learn that appropriate behavior (walk, do not run) contributes to a safe, orderly environment.

***Directed Lesson:***

1. ***Establish the Need:*** The teacher will establish the need by saying: **"Boys and girls, we must have rules in our classroom. These rules will help us to learn and to keep our classroom safe."**

2. ***Introduction:*** The teacher will read the book <u>Peter Rabbit</u> or select another story with a similar story plot. After reading the story, discuss it and have the children verbally demonstrate an awareness of the importance of rules:

   ▶ listening to rules
   ▶ obeying the rules
   ▶ learning consequences for not obeying the rules

   After the discussion, the teacher will say: **"If the rules of our classroom are not followed, you will be given one reminder."** For example: **"Juan, running in the classroom is against our class rules. Can you tell me why?"** If the child has difficulty remembering, solicit the help of another child.

   If a rule is broken after a reminder, the teacher will then say: **"If you disobey the rules of our classroom, you will have to have Time Out."**

   **NOTE:** As the school year progresses and children become familiar with their class rules, fewer reminders should be given as well as Time Outs.

   The teacher will use hand puppets to identify the following skills. Patterns for puppets are provided on pages xii through xvii.

3. ***Identify the Skill Components:*** (list on board)

   1. Listen to directions.
   2. Follow classroom rules.
   3. Help your neighbor (classmate).

4. ***Model the Skill: Walk, Do Not Run, In the Classroom.*** The teacher will model the skill with flannel board cut-outs or a puppet. Demonstrate on the flannel board how the figure (person, animal) *slowly* goes from one side to the opposite side, and then returns.

1

Then demonstrate how the figure *rapidly* goes from one side to the opposite side and: steps and falls, or bumps into the wall, or bumps into a person.

Teacher then states that because the figure broke a classroom rule (no running), he must take the consequences—Time Out for five minutes.

At this time the teacher puts the figure in a Time Out area on the flannel board and says **"I did not follow the rules, but I will be more careful the next time."**

5. **Behavioral Rehearsal:**

   A. *Selection:* The teacher chooses small groups to role play.

   B. *Role Play:* Each group will practice disciplinary skills being taught.

   C. *Completion:* After each role play, reinforce correct behavior and identify inappropriate behavior. Re-enact role play with corrections. If there are no corrections, role play is complete.

   D. *Reinforcers:* The teacher will remind the children: **"Try to obey the rules so you do not have to go to the Time Out chair. But if you do have to go to Time Out, take your consequences like a good sport. You are a good boy/girl!"**

   E. *Discussion:* The teacher can tell the children how important it is to have a safe room. Have the children identify appropriate behaviors and tell what might happen if these behaviors are not followed in the room. (Prompting from the teacher may be necessary.)

6. *Practice:* Take the children for a slow walk and point out, as well as having children point out, things that might happen if they ran (e.g., fall on broken glass, get hit by a car). Reinforce the appropriate way to walk.

7. *Independent Use:* The children will practice and use the skill daily throughout the year during normal activities. The teacher will reinforce and praise continually. (**"I like the way Johnny _____."**)

8. *Continuation:* This skill will be continued throughout the year. The teacher can make a crown from tagboard or a medallion on a string that children who remember the rules earn the right to wear. The following page provides a reproducible pattern for a social skills medallion.

## SOCIAL SKILL
### *Avoiding Uncontrolled Negative Behavior*

**Behavioral Objective:** The children will learn controlled positive behavior, to assure an environment conducive to learning and living.

**Directed Lesson:**

1.  **Establish the Need:** The purpose of the lesson is to provide appropriate disciplinary action when necessary by taking away or adding activities which the student enjoys (positive/negative reinforcement).

2.  **Introduction:** **"Children, you all know that it is very important to have rules and regulations for proper behavior in the classroom. We also have to have something called DISCIPLINARY ACTION for those children who do not follow the rules."** Now tell the children the following story:

    > **"There was once a boy named John. He was a kindergartner who knew all the rules but had one big problem. He didn't follow the rules. One day he ran fast across the room. Because he broke the rule, he had to stay in Time Out for five minutes. It seemed like forever. John sat there while the rest of the class was having fun learning so many new things and playing new games."**

    After the story, the teacher discusses why we need rules and consequences, so that the rules are followed.

3.  **Identify the Skill Components:** Present specific classroom rules to the children, for example:

    > 1. Walk, do not run, in the classroom.
    > 2. Speak in a quiet voice.
    > 3. Be a good listener.
    > 4. Follow the teacher's directions.
    > 5. Share during play time.

    Next, post this progressive use of consequences for breaking the rules on a large chart. Use a hand puppet to identify each one for the children:

    > ▶ Time Out corner.
    > ▶ Ban from certain centers, games or activities

4

- ❱ Name on the board
- ❱ Note home
- ❱ Principal's office

4. ***Model the Skill:*** Teacher explains the skill. This should be done in several lessons that review the rules and show the consequences if the rules are not followed.

5. ***Behavioral Rehearsal:***

    A. *Selection:* Teacher selects several children to demonstrate.

    B. *Role Play:* Have children play their assigned roles (e.g., running in the classroom, resulting in Time Out for five minutes). Develop disciplinary strategies for each rule with the students and the skills needed to follow the rules.

    C. *Completion:* After each role play, reinforce correct behavior and identify inappropriate behaviors. Re-enact role play with corrections. If there are no corrections, role play is complete.

    D. *Reinforcers:* During the role play, the teacher will use verbal and non-verbal praise and expressions of approval to develop the children's understanding and elicit appropriate responses. In order to maintain the appropriate behavior, the teacher should remember to regularly praise and express appreciation to the class for practicing self-control.

    E. *Discussion:* The teacher will ask the children to describe what they learned from the role-play about rules and consequences.

6. ***Practice:*** To maintain and reinforce this skill, children's names can be put on large apple shapes and the "apples" pinned to a large tree chart. If a child breaks a rule, his/her apple "gets loose" from the tree and begins to "fall" from the tree. With each level, privileges are lost. If the apple "hits the ground," the principal or parent is notified. Return all apples to the top of the tree daily for a fresh start.

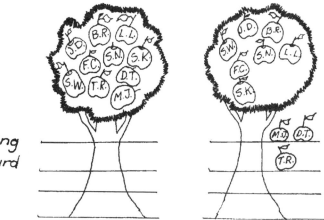

verbal warning
name on board
time out
call parent

7. ***Independent Use:*** Children will take home a letter explaining disciplinary actions for their behavior in school. (A sample letter is provided on the next page.) Parents are asked to reinforce the results of the positive/negative behavior at home. The letter should be returned with an adult's signature.

8. ***Continuation:*** Teacher will tell the children to remember to learn the skills that avoid behavior that requires DISCIPLINARY ACTION. Continue to point out the need for these skills as related situations arise throughout the year.

Dear Family:

I am learning to keep the rules established in my classroom. These are the skills required to follow the rules: (Below are sample skills. Make up skills to follow the rules that fit your classroom.)

1. Walk. Do not run.
2. Speak in a quiet voice.
3. Be a good listener.
4. Follow the teacher's directions.
5. Share during play time.
6. Put things away when finished.
7. Ask, if not knowing what to do.
8. Raise hand before asking a question, if in a group.
9. Do not disturb others during work time.
10. Finish "do now" work now.

When we break the rules, the consequences are (listed in order of increased severity):

1. Time out for five minutes.
2. Ban from certain centers, games or activities.
3. Name on the board.
4. Note home.
5. Principal's office.

Will you please sign my note so that I can return it to my teacher?

Thank you,

_____

Child

_____

Parent Signature

Name: _____  Room: _____  Date: _____

# SOCIAL SKILL

## *Fully Understanding the Situation Before Taking Action*

**Behavioral Objective:** The children will learn to think of all the reasons responsible for creating the situation or conflict before taking action.

**Directed Lesson:**

1.  **Establish the Need:** The purpose is to understand the reasons (both physical and psychological) for the problem so as not to attack the person but the problem.

2.  **Introduction:** The teacher says:

    **"I am going to tell you a story about a little girl named Beth. This is Beth (show the picture of Beth on the accompanying worksheet for Lesson 3). Today was picture-taking day at her school. The teacher told the children that she was going to line them up according to height. It was Beth's turn to get in line, and the teacher asked her to get in front of Sara. Sara did not listen to the teacher's explanation and, when Beth stepped in front of her, Sara pushed Beth out of line."**

    **"Why do you think this happened? Did Sara understand the situation?"**

    After discussing the story and why it happened, emphasize to the children the importance of understanding the situation before acting.

3.  **Identify the Skill Components:** The teacher uses a hand puppet to help the children understand the skills involved in understanding situations before taking action. List the following skill components on a large chart:

    1. Think before you act.
    2. Think of the correct way to act.
    3. Remember the rules.
    4. Remember the consequences of your actions.
    5. If you don't understand the situation, ask/tell the teacher.

4.  **Model the Skill:** Teacher and students act out an accidental "bump." Teacher and students apologize.

**5.** **Behavioral Rehearsal:**

    A. *Selection:* Teacher asks one child at a time to participate in the role play.

    B. *Role Play:* The participants are assigned their roles or the situations they will role play.

    C. *Completion:* After each role play, reinforce correct behavior, identify inappropriate behaviors, and re-enact role play with corrections.

    D. *Reinforcers:* During the role playing, the teacher will use verbal rewards and expressions of praise to provide reinforcement. Praise and appreciation should be used often throughout the school year to maintain the skill.

    E. *Discussion:* The teacher can discuss with the class the manner in which the children role played and allow children to point out any undesirable behaviors.

**6.** **Practice:** Teacher will give each child a copy of the accompanying worksheet and explain that the worksheet has a picture of Beth before she got into the line. On the right side are two faces. Direct children to color the face that shows how Beth would have looked if Sara had understood the situation and had not pushed her.

**7.** **Independent Use:** Teacher will initiate a class discussion about understanding situations before acting at home. He or she will ask children the following questions:

    A. **"Did you ever take action before you fully understood a situation at home?"**

    B. **"What did you do?"**

    C. **"Did you or someone else get hurt or into trouble?"**

    D. **"Did you behave in a good way?"**

**8.** **Continuation:** The teacher will tell children, **"Always fully understand the situation before taking action. Remember, the key is to think and then act."** Continue pointing out the need for this skill as related situations arise.

Reminder: **"Use your *words* to settle problems."**

Name _____   Date _____

# SOCIAL SKILL
## *Being a Good Listener*

*Behavioral Objective:* The children will listen and participate in group activities.

*Directed Lesson:*

1.  *Establish the Need:* The teacher will establish the need by telling children that it is important to listen to what other people say because this is one way we learn. Everyone wants to learn.

2.  *Introduction:* **"Today we are going to LISTEN with our ears."** (Say this in a hushed tone, and cup hands around ears.)

    Sit in a circle with legs crossed and hands clasped on ankles. Have students close their eyes and listen to the sounds around them without saying a word.

    (In hushed tone) **"When I count to three, slowly open your eyes. Ready . . . one, two, three. Raise your hand if you heard something."** Allow children to respond appropriately, for example, "Someone sneezed" or "I heard the clock ticking."

    Next, explain that they are going to close their eyes again (no peeking) and you are going to make three sounds for them to hear. **"All eyes closed. Just listen, do not call out. Here is the first sound** (ring a bell); **here is the second sound** (beat a drum); **here is the last sound** (clap your hands). **When I count to three, slowly open your eyes. Ready, one, two, three."**

    Encourage children to tell what they heard. Then, with their eyes open so they can observe, Teacher can repeat each of the three sounds.

    Show children the following: When hands are clapped together a sound is made. When fingertips are clapped together, no sound is made. Practice clapping hands, and tapping finger tips. (Clap three times, tap three times, repeat.)

    Play a record so that children can listen to the song, and tap fingers or clap hands in time to the music, following the direction of the teacher.

3.  *Identify the Skill Components:* (list on board)

    1. Sit quietly. No talking.
    2. Look at the person speaking.
    3. Listen carefully to what is being said.
    4. Try to understand what has been said.

> 5. Remember what has been said.

4. ***Model the Skill:*** The teacher models the skill by asking one child to do one specific task. The child will repeat what has been said and perform the given task.

5. ***Behavioral Rehearsal:***

   A. *Selection:* The teacher divides the class into small groups.

   B. *Role Play:* The teacher assigns a task to each group by telling one member of the group what the group should do or say when it is their turn to perform.

       Examples:
   - telling what they had for breakfast or lunch
   - telling their favorite food
   - telling (and showing) the class how and when to cross the street
   - telling (and showing) the class how to form a line
   - telling why it is necessary to listen to important sounds such as footsteps behind you or someone talking

   C. *Completion:* After each role play, have the children applaud. The children in the audience should also try to repeat as many things as they remember from what the students said in the role play.

   D. *Reinforcers:* Reinforce appropriate behavior with verbal praise, tangible rewards, group reinforcement, and non-verbal praise (a smile or a pat on the back).

   E. *Discussion:* Children will play a game called "Body Parts." Make sure that you use only the body parts they are familiar with.

       To play the game, all stand in a circle:

   **"Make sure that you LISTEN to me. Do what I <u>say</u>, not what I <u>do</u>. Ready?"**
   **"Put your hands on your head."** (Teacher puts her hands on her head.)
   **"Are your hands on your head? Good listeners! Let's try it again."**
   **"Put your hands on your head."** (Teacher puts her hands on her hips.)
   **"Are your hands on your head? Good listeners! Let's try again."**

   (Continue with additional directions.)
   Praise good listeners.
   Reinforce others.

6. ***Practice:*** Read a good story to the children, then go back through the pictures and have children identify one item in each illustration that actually makes a sound. Use: Carle, Eric, *The Mixed-Up Chameleon* (New York: Harper Collins Children's Books, 1984).

7. ***Independent Use:*** Children will listen during group activities while others talk. Selected children will repeat what they heard.

**8.    *Continuation:***

(A)   Have children listen for things they can hear on their way to school, e.g., fire engine, car horn, birds singing, etc.

(B)   Go for a "Listening Walk" on the playground. What do we hear?

# SOCIAL SKILL
## *Ability to Sit and Listen Quietly*

**Behavioral Objective:** The children will be able to sit and listen quietly to a speaker.

**Directed Lesson:**

1.  **Establish the Need:** The teacher will establish the importance of listening with the following comments: **"Boys and girls, it is very important to learn to listen when people are talking. If people do not listen when other people are talking then they will never learn anything or know how to do anything."**

2.  **Introduction:** **"We are going to do something that will help you to learn to listen. Let's get ready. First, sit up straight and put your hands in your lap. Second, look at me and keep your lips closed. I am going to tell you a story and while I am talking I will be watching to see if you know how to behave when you are listening."**

    The teacher then tells the following story, observing the children to see if they are practicing the appropriate behaviors.

    > **"One day Johnny went to the beach with his mother, his father, and his little sister. Johnny and his sister played in the water and dug in the sand. When they were hungry they ate a delicious lunch that their father had made. When it was almost dark, they had to go home. Johnny's mother promised them that they would come to the beach again."**

    After telling the story, the teacher will give verbal and non-verbal praise and expressions of approval to the children she observed listening. She will encourage those who did not quite succeed to try harder.

3.  **Identify the Skill Components:** (list on the board)

    The teacher uses a hand puppet to identify the components of this skill:

    1.  Sit quietly.
    2.  Place hands in lap.
    3.  Look at speaker.
    4.  Listen to speaker.
    5.  Keep lips sealed.

4.  **Model the Skill:** The teacher will single out students who practiced the 5 listening skills.

She will invite two of these students to come to where she is seated and will re-read the story while they model their five listening skills for their classmates to observe.

**5.** ***Behavioral Rehearsal:***

        A. *Selection:* The teacher selects two children to role play.

        B. *Role Play:* Teacher asks one child to tell the story and asks the other child to demonstrate the correct behaviors. Repeat the role play with other children, as attention permits.

        C. *Completion:* After each role play, reinforce correct behavior, identify inappropriate behaviors, and re-enact role play with corrections. If there are no corrections, role play is complete.

        D. *Reinforcers:* Use verbal praise, tangible rewards, group reinforcement, and non-verbal praise, such as a wink, pat or smile. Also, use the Good Listener Rabbit award on the next page.

        E. *Discussion:* Teacher announces that she/he will give recognition and appreciation for the continued practice of the appropriate behavior regularly during the school year.

**6.** ***Practice:*** Read a short story and ask students simple questions such as the names of the main characters.

**7.** ***Independent Use:*** The children will make a "good listener" head band from construction paper and large cut-outs of rabbit ears. They can wear their head bands as visual reminders during quiet work time or quiet story time.

The good listener hats can be stored in a magic container. When the lid is open, it gets *very* quiet in the room.

The rabbit ears are sensitive to noise and may need to go back into the container if someone continues to use his/her loud voice.

**8.** ***Continuation:*** The teacher should continue to remind children of the need for this skill as related situations arise, using catchy phrases such as:

**"Good manners are always in style"** or

**"Good manners never go out of style"** or

**"*Be* a good friend and you will *have* many friends"** or

> **"If I'm kind to you**
> **If you're kind to me**
> **What good friends**
> **We'll always be."**

Name:

_____

# Good Listener

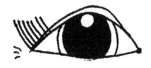 

1. Sit quietly.
2. Hands in lap.
3. Look at speaker.
4. Listen to speaker.
5. Keep lips sealed.

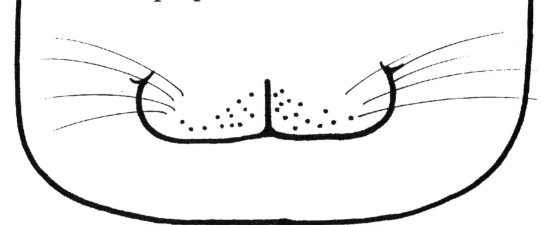

## SOCIAL SKILL

### *Ability to Listen/Participate in Class Discussion*

**Behavioral Objective:** The children will be able to listen/participate in a class listening and discussion activity by raising their hand to speak and waiting to be called on before speaking.

**Directed Lesson:**

1. **Establish the Need:** Teacher establishes the need by initiating a discussion that builds upon the previous listening lesson. In order for people to talk together they must raise their hands to speak and wait for their turn before they speak.

2. **Introduction:** The teacher states **"I am going to read and tell you a story. When I have finished, I am going to ask you questions about the story to see how well you listened and how well you know how to speak to the class about what you heard."**

   The teacher selects and reads a children's literature book that deals with the topic of listening, for example *Horace,* by Holly Keller, and *Miss Nelson is Missing,* by James Marshall. Discuss the story.

   After the story has been read, the children are reminded of the behaviors that demonstrate the ability to participate in a discussion. The teacher then asks questions about the story and calls on children to answer.

   The teacher reinforces the behavior of those children who demonstrate the skill by calling on them and stating **"_____, you raised your hand! Good! Can you tell us . . . ?"** The teacher expresses the expectation that all the children will be able to learn and practice good listening and participation skills.

3. **Identify the Skill Components:** (list on a colorful chart and hang in the room)

   The teacher identifies the following skill components:

   1. Sit quietly.
   2. Place hands in lap or near body.
   3. Look at speaker.
   4. Listen to speaker.
   5. Raise hand to speak.
   6. Wait for turn to speak.
   7. Answer the question.

4. ***Model the Skill:*** The teacher asks the children to watch as she/he models the skill by sitting and listening to a tape recorded message. The children are asked to observe and agree that all the components of the skill were demonstrated.

5. ***Behavioral Rehearsal:***
   A. *Selection:* The teacher asks one child to come to the front and be the teacher.
   B. *Role Play:* The child will hold the book while a record or tape plays or "reads" a familiar story. Before beginning, the child names as many listening skill components as possible for the other children to demonstrate. After presenting the story, the "teacher" is reminded to choose only those children who know how to listen and participate in a discussion to answer questions about the tape or story message.
   C. *Completion:* After each role play, reinforce correct behavior, identify inappropriate behaviors, and reenact role play with corrections. If there are no corrections, role play is complete.
   D. *Reinforcers:* Use verbal praise, tangible rewards, group reinforcement, and non-verbal praise (e.g., hug, pat, smile) to recognize correct behavior.
   E. *Discussion:* Discuss why it is important to participate in class discussions (to show understanding, to share information, to learn what someone is thinking).

6. ***Practice:*** In small group activities, three or four children can sit at a listening station with their headphones on listening to the story "The Three Billy Goats Gruff" (use a tape or record). After the story is completed, ask three or four simple questions about the story, for example:

   1. How many goats were there?
   2. Who lived under the bridge?
   3. Where were the goats going?

   The good listeners can be given a smile face button (paper) that says "I am a good listener."

   Distribute copies of the "Three Billy Goats Gruff" worksheet that accompanies this lesson and direct children to color the worksheet.

7. ***Independent Use:*** Praise and appreciation should be given repeatedly during the school year to strengthen and maintain the skill.

8. ***Continuation:*** Teacher tells the children that the more carefully they listen to others, the better others will listen to them. Continue pointing out the need for this skill as related situations arise.

Name _____

Date _____

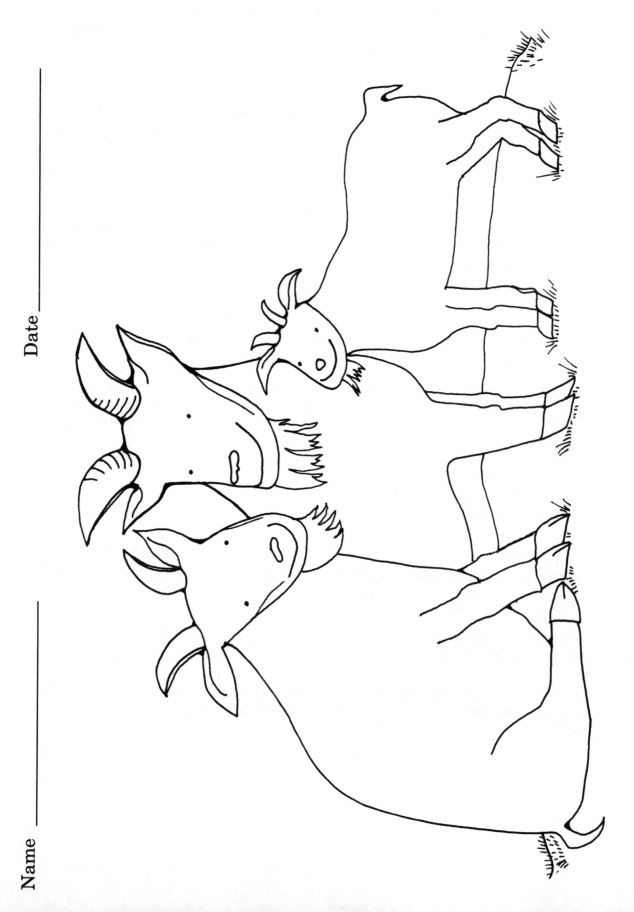

# FOLLOWING RULES

## SOCIAL SKILL

### *Recognizing the Importance of Classroom Rules*

***Behavioral Objective:*** The children will learn the importance of following rules.

***Directed Lesson:***

1. ***Establish the Need:*** The teacher will establish the need for classroom rules by stating: **"We must have rules in our room so we know how to behave."**

2. ***Introduction:*** **"Today we will talk about rules. Rules help us. Rules tell us what we can or cannot do. There are several kinds of rules:**

   1. **When you are home, you must follow the rules at home. This means you must do what adults at home tell you to do.**

   2. **When you come into the building, you must follow the rules that are used in the building. (Ex.: Walk, do not run, in the halls.)**

   3. **When you come into our room, you must follow our room rules. (Ex.: Hang up your coat.)**

   **Today we are going to talk about the rules that we are going to use in our class-room."**

   Teacher explains each rule and uses puppets where appropriate.

   *Suggested Rules*

   1. When the teacher puts out the lights, FREEZE. Stand still or sit quietly as a statue and listen for directions.

   2. Use indoor voices (quiet voices).

   3. Walk, do not run, in the room.

   4. Be a good helper.

   5. Put things back where they belong.

   6. Assist your neighbor (classmate).

3. ***Identify the Skill Components:*** (list on board)

   1. Sit quietly.
   2. Listen to the person explaining the rules.
   3. Say and learn the rules.
   4. Obey the rules.

5. Be cooperative.

6. Be helpful.

4. ***Model the Skill:*** The teacher will demonstrate or select one child to act out the skill components needed to follow the rules.

5. ***Behavioral Rehearsal:***

    A. *Selection:* The teacher will divide the children into as many groups as there are classroom rules or skill components.

    B. *Role Play:* (Role play can be continued for one week.) There should be four or six groups and four or six rules. Each group should have the opportunity to role play each rule by using the skill components. While one group plays, the others will be the audience, reversing roles until all the children have completed at least one role play. (Day One complete.)

    Repeat the same activity for the next three or four days or until all the children have role played all the rules.

    C. *Continuation:* After each role play, reinforce correct behavior and identify inappropriate behavior. Re-enact role play with corrections. After each role play, the audience will applaud.

    D. *Reinforcers:* Occasionally when a teacher sees a child obeying one of the classroom rules, she will verbally compliment the child saying, **"Virginia, I'm so glad that you remembered to . . . "**

    E. *Discussion:* Until the rules are familiar to the children, the teacher should talk about each classroom rule that the children seem to be forgetting. This can be done when class begins, and again before dismissal.

6. ***Practice:*** The children will practice the rules daily during classroom activities. Also, the teacher may choose a game or activity. For example: **"Today is whisper day. The only way we can talk is if we whisper."** Continually remind them to whisper. At the end of the day, the teacher may want to reward children for obeying the rule.

7. ***Independent Use:*** The teacher will initiate a whole class discussion (at least once a week for about five minutes) that will reinforce the rules by allowing the children to recall how they have or have not obeyed the rules in the classroom, in the building, or in their home.

8. ***Continuation:*** The rules should be reviewed each day and children encouraged to practice the rules every day throughout the year.

**NOTE:** The same lesson can be used to have the children tell about their rules at home and why they think these rules are necessary.

## SOCIAL SKILL
### *Following Directions During Instruction and Clean-Up*

***Behavioral Objective:*** Children will learn to follow directions during instruction and clean-up time.

***Directed Lesson:***

1. ***Establish the Need:*** The teacher should explain the meaning of directions: **"Directions tell us how to do something."** Explain that if you do not listen to the teacher's directions, you will not be able to do your work.

2. ***Introduction:*** **"Today we are going to talk about following directions."** The teacher will tell a story about a child who did not follow directions.

   **"Curtis: The Boy Who Did Not Like To Follow Directions**

   **"Curtis was a little boy who did not like to follow directions. Curtis would play around while the teacher was giving directions to the class. He did not hear the directions that were being given by his teacher. When it was time to do his work, Curtis did not know what to do. He could not understand why his classmates were enjoying doing their work and why his classmates could complete their work each day.**

   **"The boys and girls who had completed their work got cookies. Curtis did not get any cookies because he did not listen to his teacher's directions and could not complete his work."**

   After telling the story, the teacher asks several questions to involve the children in the lesson.

3. ***Identify the Skill Components:*** (list on board)

   1. Look at the person giving directions.
   2. Listen to the directions.
   3. Remember the directions.
   4. Follow the directions.

4. ***Model the Skill:*** The teacher will play simple games to give directions which he/she then carries out.

5. ***Behavioral Rehearsal:***

   A. *Selection:* The teacher selects children, one at a time, to role play.

23

B. *Role Play:* The teacher will direct selected students the play the direction game:

    1. Please pick up a ball and bounce it three times.

    2. Please place a block on the shelf (in the block center).

    3. Please bring a pencil to the teacher.

    4. Please pick up a piece of scrap paper from the floor and put it in the wastebasket.

    5. Please go to the door and close (open) it.

C. *Completion:* After each role play, reinforce correct behavior, identify inappropriate behaviors, and re-enact role play with corrections. If there are no corrections, role play is complete.

D. *Reinforce:* The teacher gives non-verbal praise and expressions of approval to children for appropriate responses.

E. *Discussion:* Children will discuss how important it is to follow directions.

6. ***Practice:*** In small groups, give children the following directions: **"Go to the chalkboard and draw a smiling face on the board."** Children who follow directions will be praised and rewarded with a sticker to wear.

7. ***Independent Use:*** In order to practice listening to a set of directions, have students color the accompanying worksheet using the colors assigned by the teacher. The teacher will then evaluate the finished product of each child. If the children follow the directions correctly, place a star on the worksheet.

8. ***Continuation:*** Teacher tells children that using this skill each and every day will help them to feel good inside and to do well in school.

**NOTE:** Use this same format for another lesson on cleaning up toys in the classroom.

*Suggested Reading* (Listening and following directions)

dePaola, Tomie. *Strega Nona*. Morristown, NJ: Silver Burdett, 1991.

McKissack, Patricia. *Flossie and the Fox*. New York: Dial Books for Young Readers, 1986

Name _____ Date _____

## SOCIAL SKILL
### Following Oral Directions

*Behavioral Objective:* The children, depending upon their own ability, will be able to follow one, two, or three oral direction(s) upon request.

*Directed Lesson:*

1.  *Establish the Need:* Teacher establishes the need for following directions with these comments: **"Boys and girls, it is very important to be able to do what you are asked to do. This is called <u>following instructions</u> or <u>following directions</u>. If you do not follow directions, that is, do what you are asked to do by your teacher or parent, you sometimes may cause accidents or get yourself into trouble. When you are going to follow directions, you must look at the person who is talking to you, listen to that person so that you will know what to do, then you must do what they have told you to do."**

2.  *Introduction:* **"Now I am going to tell you a story about a little girl who did not follow the directions her mother gave her. She did not do what her mother asked her to do."** (Use hand puppets if available.)

    **"Once there was a little girl named Susie who wanted to play in her yard with her puppy. Her mother said that she could, but she told Susie to remember to close and lock the gate so the puppy could not run away. When Susie went into the yard with her puppy she forgot to close and lock the gate. Soon her little puppy went through the open gate and ran away down the street. Susie began to cry and called for her mother to help her catch the puppy. Her mother came and ran out of the gate. A big boy helped them to catch the puppy before it got lost or hurt. Mother thanked the nice big boy and then she said to Susie, 'You didn't follow my directions. You did not do what I asked you to do. I am glad your puppy is safe and I know that from now on you will remember to listen and follow my directions.'"**

    After telling the story, the teacher asks several questions to involve the children in the lesson.

    **NOTE:** Other appropriate stories include various versions of *Little Red Riding Hood* and *Lon Po Po: A Red Riding Hood Story from China*, by Ed Young (New York: Philomel Books, 1989).

3.  *Identify the Skill Components:* (list on board)

    The teacher uses a hand puppet to identify the components of the skill.

1. Look at the person giving directions.
2. Listen to the directions.
3. Carry out the directions.
4. Clean up immediately after completing an activity.

4.    ***Model the Skill:*** The teacher uses the hand puppet to give directions which she then carries out.

5.    ***Behavioral Rehearsal:***

   A. *Selection:* The teacher selects one child to role play.

   B. *Role Play:* Child will be told by the teacher to please:

   1. Put a pencil on the desk.
   2. Pick up a piece of paper and throw it away.
   3. Go to the chalkboard, pick up a piece of chalk, and draw a line.
      Another idea is a sequencing game where students first have to touch one body part, repeat this, and then add another, etc. For example: (1) Touch your nose. (2) Touch your nose, then touch your shoulders, and so on.

   C. *Completion:* After each role play, reinforce correct behavior, identify inappropriate behaviors, and re-enact role play with corrections. If there are no corrections, role play is complete.

   D. *Reinforcers:* The teacher gives verbal and non-verbal praise and expressions of approval to the children for appropriate responses.

   E. *Discussion:* Children will discuss how important it is to follow directions.

6.    ***Practice:*** Give children the following directions in groups of two or four: **"Go to the math shelf, take out the bead box, then choose beads to make a necklace."** Children who follow directions may then make a necklace to wear until clean-up time.

7.    ***Independent Use:*** To give children practice in listening to a set of directions, the teacher will give them copies of the accompanying worksheet and direct them to color the worksheet using the colors assigned by the teacher. Evaluation of good listening skills will be assessed by the teacher after observing the finished product. Children can take their colored worksheets home to their families.

8.    ***Continuation:*** Teacher tells children **"If you use this skill whenever and wherever you need it, you will prevent many problems and learn more quickly in school."** Teacher should continue pointing out the need for this skill as related situations arise.

Name _____    Date _____

## SOCIAL SKILL
*Following Clean-Up Directions*

***Behavioral Objective:*** The children will follow directions enabling them to clean up following an activity.

***Directed Lesson:***

1. ***Establish the Need:*** The teacher establishes the need for following directions to put away materials after completing an activity with the following comments. **"Children, it is very important that you learn how to clean up and put away your work after you have finished it. If you do not clean up and put away your work, the area will not be ready for someone else to use. We would also have a very messy classroom."**

2. ***Introduction:*** Teacher says:

   **"I will tell you a story about a little boy who had a very messy room. His clothes were everywhere and he never replaced his toys in his toybox or put his book, papers and crayons on his shelf. He was always upset because he could never find his shoes when it was time to go out. Many times he cried because he'd lost favorite toys in all the mess.**

   **One day his mother said that she was tired of helping him to find things. 'If you don't start to keep your room neat and clean,' she said, 'I will sweep up and throw everything away. If you will promise to try to keep it in order, I will help you to clean it up so that you can find everything.'**

   **The little boy promised his mother that he would begin to put his things in the proper place, and she helped him to clean his room. He was very happy to be able to find his shoes and his favorite toys whenever he wanted them. He was also happy that his mother would not have to sweep up and throw away his toys."**

   After telling the story, the teacher initiates a discussion with the children about the little boy. He/she encourages them to compare themselves to the little boy and relates the story to their classroom by pointing out how important it is to also have a neat classroom.

3. ***Identify the Skill components:*** (list on board)

   The teacher identifies the following skill components for the children:

   > 1. Look at the person giving the directions.

2. Listen to the directions.

3. Carry out the directions.

4. Clean up immediately after completing an activity.

4.   ***Model the Skill:*** The teacher has at hand several activities from the shelves in the room. Using a system that matches a symbol (shape, design, animal, etc.) on the box with a corresponding symbol on the shelf, the teacher demonstrates how to look on the container for the symbol, then look on the shelf for the same symbol and place the container in the correct location.

5.   ***Behavioral Rehearsal:***

A. *Selection:* The teacher selects several children to role play.

B. *Role Play:* Students go to the shelves and remove an activity. They return to the group with their selected items and give them to another child to put away in the proper location. Repeat giving children different roles.

C. *Completion:* After each role play, reinforce correct behavior, identify inappropriate behaviors, and re-enact role play with corrections. If there are no corrections, role play is complete.

D. *Reinforcers:* Reinforce appropriate behaviors with verbal praise, tangible rewards, group reinforcement, and non-verbal praise such as a pat or a smile.

E. *Discussion:* Teacher asks children what they learned from the role play about following directions.

6.   ***Practice:*** To maintain and reinforce the skill a list of the children's names could be kept in such areas as the blocks or housekeeping corner. When the children demonstrate their ability to clean up these areas, they can receive a sticker of some sort beside their names. After they receive five stickers, they can be given a reward (selecting the book to be read aloud, first to line up, etc.).

7.   ***Independent Use:*** Children may take home a note such as that on the following page explaining that they are learning to clean up and put their things in the correct location. The parents are asked to select three or four items, show the child where they belong, and instruct the child to return them to their proper location. The next day children can discuss their home experiences at school.

8.   ***Continuation:*** Teacher tells children, **"If you use this skill whenever and wherever you need it, you will usually be able to find things when you need them much more easily."** Teacher should continue pointing out the need for this skill as related situations arise.

Date: _____

Child's
Name _____

Dear Family:

I am learning to keep my classroom neat and clean. Will you help me to be neat and clean at home?

Please take out three (3) kitchen items, such as spoon, pan, bowls or other things we use at home. Put them around the room, and be sure to tell me where they belong.

Now, watch me! I will show you that I can put them all back where they belong.

When I have cleaned up nicely, will you please sign my note so that I can return it to my teacher? Thank You!

_____

(Parent Signature)

## SOCIAL SKILL

### *Using Courtesy Words "Please," "May I," and "Thank You"*

**Behavioral Objective:** The children will learn to have respect for others by using the courtesy words "Please," "May I," and "Thank you."

**Directed Lesson:**

1. **Establish the Need:** The teacher will explain to the children that by being courteous to others, it gives them a good feeling when they help you. Persons will be more willing to help you if you are polite when you ask them and if you let them know that you are happy after they have helped you.

2. **Introduction:** "Today we are going to learn some polite magic words. These magic words are words that we should use when we are asking for help or asking for permission to use something that belongs to someone else. We will do this three times (hold up three fingers).

   ONE (hold up one finger)
      The first polite words are "May I." Say them with me: 'May I.' (Very good.)
      Listen carefully:
         *May I* use the red crayon?
         *May I* play on the swings?
         *May I* wash my hands now?
      Use *May I* when you are asking for something.

   TWO (hold up two fingers)
      The second polite word is "Please." Say it with me: 'Please.' (Very good.)
      Listen carefully:
         *Please* help me put away the blocks.
         *Please* put the books away.
         *Please* get your coat.
      Use *please* when you want help.

   THREE (hold up three fingers)
      The third set of polite words are "Thank you." Say it with me: 'Thank you.' (Very good.)
      Listen carefully:
         *When* someone gives you a present, say *Thank you.*
         *When* someone lets you ahead of them in line, say *Thank you.*
      Say *thank you* when someone does something nice just for you.

**Review:** **"'May I' and 'Please' are special words. They make someone else feel good when you asked them for permission or for help.**
**When someone helps you, you say 'Thank you.' The words 'Thank you' let another person know that you are happy that they gave you something or did something for you. Let's remember to use our magic words: 'Please,' 'May I,' and 'Thank you.'"**

3.    ***Identify the Skill Components:*** (list on board)

      1. Think before you speak.

      2. Use the words "May I" and/or "Please" when you ask for permission to do or to take something.

      3. Use the word "Please" when you need help.

      4. Use the words "May I" when you want something.

      5. Wait for the person to give you what you asked for or the permission to do what you asked and wanted to do.

      6. Say "Thank you" after you get something or after someone does something for you.

4.    ***Model the Skill:*** The teacher will use hand puppets to demonstrate the skill. Have the puppets ask a child to please get something. When the child gives the puppets the requested object, the puppets will say "Thank you" to the child.

5.    ***Behavioral Rehearsal:***

      A. *Selection:* Teacher selects two children to role play.

      B. *Role Play:* Give one child an object and have the second child ask for it using the proper skills of saying "Please" and/or "May I" when asking for the object and saying "Thank you" when the object is received.

      C. *Completion:* After each role play, reinforce the correct action and identify inappropriate action. Re-enact role play with corrections. If there are no corrections, role play is complete.

      D. *Reinforcers:* Verbal praise, tangible rewards, group reinforcement and non-verbal praise (hug, pat on head) may be used when child uses correct skills.

      E. *Discussion:* After the role-plays are complete, the teacher asks the children, **"What magic words did we learn today?"** (Children respond: "May I, Please, and Thank you.") The teacher asks, **"Why do we use these words?"** (Children respond: "They make us feel good when we do something for others and they make others feel good when they do something for us.")

6.    ***Practice:*** Give each child a blank sheet of paper and give one child all the crayons. Children are reminded that they must use the magic words to obtain a crayon. Once children have received a crayon, ask them to draw a happy picture.

7.  ***Independent Use:*** The children will use the courtesy words in the classroom when appropriate. The teacher will give praise when he/she hears the children use the skills they have learned. Remind the children to use these words at home and everywhere they go.

8.  ***Continuation:*** As a role model for the children, reinforce the use of courtesy words by using them frequently and by putting emphasis on the courtesy words.

    *Suggested Reading* (Caring)

    Dr. Seuss. *Horton Hears a Who!* New York: Random House Books for Young Readers, 1954.

    Polacco, Patricia. *Mrs. Katz and Tush*. New York: Bantam, 1992.

    Zolotow, Charlotte. *Big Brother*. New York: Harper & Row Jr. Books, 1960, 1982 (pap.).

# MAGIC WORDS BOOKMARKS

## SOCIAL SKILL
### *Using "Please, May I" Appropriately*

***Behavioral Objective:*** The children will use the courtesy words "Please, may I" appropriately.

***Directed Lesson***

1.  ***Establish the Need:*** The teacher states that learning to be polite when we ask someone for something is very important because the person will be more willing to help us or give us the object we ask for.

2.  ***Introduction:*** The teacher then tells the story of a little boy who always snatched toys that he wanted from other people. When others complained about his behavior he always said, "I only wanted to see it," in a very whiny voice. Soon the little boy had no friends and all the children turned their backs on him and covered up their toys whenever he came near. Next, the teacher has a discussion about this story, why no one likes to play with the boy, and what he should do to get along better with playmates.

3.  ***Identify the Skill Components*** (list on board)

    The teacher uses a hand puppet to identify the following skill components:

    > 1. Stop and think when you want something.
    > 2. Use the words "Please, may I" when asking someone for something.
    > 3. Wait until the person gives permission before taking the object or toy.

4.  ***Model the Skill:*** The teacher will use two hand puppets to demonstrate the skills involved.

5.  ***Behavioral Rehearsal:***

    A. *Selection:* The teacher selects two children to role play.

    B. *Role Play:* One child is given an object and the other is instructed to ask for that object using the correct skills.

    C. *Completion:* After each role play, reinforce correct behavior, identify inappropriate behaviors, and reenact role play with corrections. If there are no corrections, role play is complete.

    D. *Reinforcers:* Use verbal praise, tangible rewards, group reinforcement, non-verbal praise (e.g., pat, smile, hug) to reinforce correct behavior.

    E. *Discussion:* After each role play identify and reinforce correct behaviors by questioning. e.g., **"Did he/she use the correct courtesy word? Did he/she wait until permission was given?"**

6. **Practice:** The teacher will play a game with the class. The children will stand in a horizontal line. The teacher stands in front of each child and gives a direction such as **"Take one giant step."** The child must say "Teacher, may I" and wait for permission before following the direction. The game is repeated until all children have had a turn.

7. **Independent Use:** Ask children to practice using courtesy words with family. Discuss the responses the children received from family members.

8. **Continuation:** Teacher will remind children, **"If you use 'Please may I' when asking for something, people will be more willing to help you"** as related situations arise.

# SOCIAL SKILL

## Using the "Magic" Words "Please" and "Thank You"

**Behavioral Objective:** The children will use the courtesy words "Please" and "Thank you" when requesting and receiving assistance.

### Directed Lesson

1. **Establish the Need:** The teacher relates this lesson to the previous lesson using the words "May I" by commenting: **"Yesterday we talked about how important it is to ask politely when we want something from someone. We know that a person is more willing to hand you something if you ask politely for it. This is also true when you need someone to help you. There are two more special, or 'magic' words that we must learn to use when we ask someone to help us or to do something for us. These words are 'Please' and 'Thank you'."**

2. **Introduction:** The teacher reads the following story:

   **"There was a little girl named Nancy who never knew how or when to use these words. When she wanted something, she said 'Gimmee!' When she needed help she never said 'Please, help me.' She only said 'Do this,' or 'Tie my shoes.' And she never said 'Thank you.' She just walked away without a word."**

   Teacher encourages discussion about the consequences of such behavior; the little girl would have no friends, no one would help her or hand anything to her, and she would soon be very unhappy if she did not learn to use the "magic" words.

3. **Identify the Skill Components** (list on board)

   The teacher uses a hand puppet to identify for the children the following components of the skill:

   1. Stop and think of what you are going to say.
   2. Say "Please" when you ask for help.
   3. Say "Thank you" when someone has given you help.

4. **Model the Skill:** The teacher uses the hand puppet to model the skill by asking several children to get items or perform small tasks, using the appropriate courtesy word.

5. **Behavioral Rehearsal:**

   A. *Selection:* The teacher selects two children to participate in the role play.

B. *Role Play:* The first child holds the hand puppet and, using the appropriate courtesy word, asks another child to give some kind of assistance. When the assistance has been given, the first child will again use the appropriate word. This role play should be repeated until all children have had a chance to role play.

C. *Completion:* After each role play, reinforce correct behavior, identify inappropriate behaviors, and reenact role play with corrections. If there are no corrections, role play is complete.

D. *Reinforcers:* Reinforce correct behavior with verbal praise, tangible rewards, group reinforcement, and nonverbal praise (i.e., pat, smile, hug).

E. *Discussion:* How do you like people saying "Please" and "Thank you" to you? How does it make you feel?

6. ***Practice:*** The teacher will ask children to tell what they think the bunny who is receiving carrots is saying to the other bunny, in the accompanying activity sheet. They will then trace the words "THANK YOU" using a crayon or pencil and color the picture.

7. ***Independent Use:*** Ask the child to use "Please" and "Thank you" at home and report back to the class.

8. ***Continuation:*** As related situations arise, the teacher will remind the children to use the "magic" words "Please" and "Thank you."

Name _____ Date _____

## SOCIAL SKILL
### *Using the Courtesy Words "Excuse Me"*

*Behavioral Objective:* The children will use the courtesy words "Excuse me" when they accidentally do something out of place and they will offer assistance and/or express concern.

### *Directed Lesson*

1. *Establish the Need:* The teacher introduces the courtesy words by pointing out that they have already learned and discussed other courtesy or "magic" words that people use to help them get along better together. Teacher adds the words "Excuse me" to this group. Teacher states that it is necessary to learn to use these words whenever they accidentally do something that hurts or bothers another person. This way that person will know that you did not mean to hurt or bother them and will not be as angry or annoyed with you. The teacher initiates a discussion by using some examples of accidents and how to resolve them by giving assistance, expressing concern or simply excusing oneself, e.g., What if you caused someone to spill milk? What if you accidentally knocked over someone's blocks? etc.

2. *Introduction:* Read the following poem to the class.

   **"As I carried a plant in a pot today,**
   **I bumped into a friend along the way.**
   **I said 'Excuse me' when I saw his shirt.**
   **On the front was a stain made from the dirt.**
   **I put down the plant to help clean the spot.**
   **I said, 'I am sorry,'**
   **And I meant it a lot!"**

   Ask: **"What nice thing did 'I' do for my friend?"**

3. *Identify the Skill Components* (list on board)

   The teacher uses a hand puppet to identify for the children the following skill components:

   1. Stop when you bump into someone.
   2. Say "Excuse me."
   3. Offer to help the person if that is needed.
   4. See if the person is all right.

4. *Model the Skill:* The teacher will remind the children to use the expression "Excuse me." Today will be a magic "Excuse Me" Day, and everyone will be listening for those polite words.

41

**5.   *Behavioral Rehearsal:***

   A. *Selection:* The teacher selects two children to role play.

   B. *Role Play:* One child "accidentally" knocks down the blocks of the other, and immediately says "Excuse me." Identify and reinforce the correct behaviors by asking questions. Repeat the role play using correct behaviors and appropriate words until all children have had a chance to role play.

   C. *Completion:* After each role play, reinforce correct behavior, identify inappropriate behaviors, and reenact role play with corrections. If there are no corrections, role play is complete.

   D. *Reinforcers:* The teacher will identify and give praise and other reinforcement to responses that provide appropriate solutions.

   E. *Discussion:* Review the use of courtesy words and how they help prevent problems from arising.

**6.   *Practice:*** Children will color the picture of a boy helping a girl to rebuild blocks in the accompanying worksheet.

**7.   *Independent Use:*** Children will be asked to think of times at home when they had an accident. Did they use any "courtesy" words? Did they help clean up the mess? What will they do if it happens again now that they know the magic word?

**8.   *Continuation:*** Teacher will remind children of the importance of excusing themselves whenever they accidentally do something undesirable.

Name

Date

## SOCIAL SKILL

### *Using "I Am Sorry" and "Excuse Me" When Appropriate*

**Behavioral Objective:** Children will learn to respect others by using the special phrases (or additional magic words) "I'm sorry" and "Excuse me" when appropriate.

**Directed Lesson:**

1.  **Establish the Need:** The teacher establishes the need for learning to respect others.

2.  **Introduction:** "**Today we are going to talk about respecting others. Respect means treating others in a fair and honest way. Respect is expressed by using the special words 'I am sorry' and 'Excuse me' to help others understand and be recognized.**"

    The teacher will give examples of when to use "I am sorry" and "Excuse me."

    Examples:     If *Harry* accidentally pushed *Joe* while getting in line, what would Harry say to Joe? (Excuse me)

    If *Susan* accidentally sprayed water on *Joanne* at the sink, what would Susan say to Joanne? (I am sorry)

    *(Substitute names of children in the class.)

    Ask different class members to give examples of incidents when they used the special words.

    The teacher will use hand puppets to identify the following skills.

3.  **Identify the Skill Components:** (list on board)

    1. Stop when you cause an accident.
    2. Say "Excuse me."
    3. Offer to help.
    4. Say "I'm sorry."

4.  **Model the Skill:** The teacher will demonstrate an incident that will require application of the skill components.

5.  **Behavioral Rehearsal:**

    A. *Selection:* The teacher will select participants to role play.
    B. *Role Play:* Selected children will role play specific assignments provided by the teacher.

      C. *Completion:* After each role play, reinforce skill components.

      D. *Reinforcers:* Teacher will encourage children to applaud and say complimentary things about classmates. "You were very good." "You did a good job." "Well done!"

      E. *Discussion:* Ask children to remind their classmates of these special words if someone forgets to say "Excuse me" or "I'm sorry."

6. **Practice:** Write "Excuse me" and "I am sorry" on placards. Flash the cards and call upon volunteers to give an example of when to use the phrases. Alternate flashing the placards and try to give each class member an opportunity to participate.

7. **Independent Use:** Teacher should draw a tally chart in a corner of the chalkboard. Whenever "Excuse me" or "I am sorry" is heard, a mark is placed on the tally chart. Marks are totaled at the end of the day.

8. **Continuation:** Teacher will remind children to practice this skill daily.

*Suggested Reading* (Friendship)

Greenfield, Eloise, *Me and Nessie*. New York: Harper Collins Children's Books, 1975.

Hallinan, P.K. *That's What a Friend Is*. Ideals, 1990.

Hughes, Shirley. *Alfie Gives a Hand*. New York: Lothrop, 1984.

Name _____ Date _____

FOLLOW THE COURTEOUS PATH

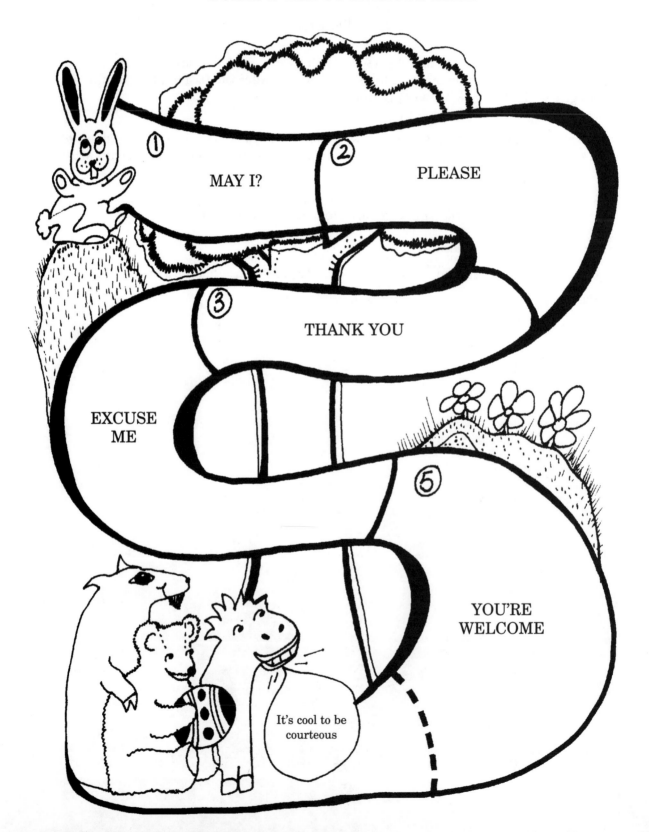

## SOCIAL SKILL
### *Feeling Good About Oneself*

***Behavioral Objective:*** The child will have a good feeling of self-worth.

***Directed Lesson:***

1. ***Establish the Need:*** The teacher establishes the need for recognizing one's own uniqueness by stating: **"There are so many ways that we are different and these differences make each one of us very special."**

2. ***Introduction:*** The teacher begins the discussion by saying: **"Let's take a look at the colors we are wearing. Look at your shoes, look at your pants, look at your shirt (etc.). OK. Raise your hand if you are wearing the color red. Good. Raise your hand if you are wearing the color blue. Good."**

   During this time, point out differences in colors, and differences in designs, such as plaids and prints.

   During this time, have students touch their hair to determine whether it is long or short, or straight or curly. Point out differences in hair color.

   The Message: Even though we look similar, we are not all quite the same. And that's just the outside. Now let's take a look at the inside. We like different colors, different toys, different games. Some of us like to paint, some would prefer to listen to a story. Some of us like to jump rope, some would rather play in the housekeeping corner.

   | | |
   |---|---|
   | Does being different make us right? | NO. |
   | Does being different make us wrong? | NO. |
   | Does being different make us OK? | YES. |

   *Suggested Reading* (Being different)

   Wildsmith, Brian. *The Little Wood Duck*. London: Oxford University Press, 1972.

   McKee David. *Elmer*. New York: Lothrop, Lee & Shephard, 1968.

   Sharmat, Marjorie. *I'm Terrific*. New York: Holiday House, 1977.

   The teacher will use hand puppets to identify the following skills.

3. ***Identify the Skill Components:*** (list on board)

   1. Think about what you have in common with others.

2. Think about something you like about yourself.

3. Think about how you are special or unique.

4. Think about something about yourself that gives you joy.

5. Say to yourself, "I am special because . . . "

4. ***Model the Skill:*** The teacher uses two dolls (from the housekeeping center), lays them on a piece of paper and draws an outline of them. (Teacher may want to trace the outline with dark felt-tip pens so children can clearly see the outline.) Teacher points out the differences in the shape of the two dolls. Have children identify the doll that goes with the outline.

5. ***Behavioral Rehearsal:***

   A. *Selection:* The teacher selects a child to lay down on a large piece of paper to have his/her outline drawn.

   B. *Role Play:* Teacher asks one child to draw another child's outline. This continues until all of the children have had their outline drawn and are able to help draw the outline of another child.

   **NOTE:** This activity will take more than one session. Older children or aides can assist.

   C. *Completion:* After each outline is drawn, teacher can cut out the outline of the body. Put the child's name on the back.

   D. *Reinforcers:* Verbal praise: tell the children how wonderful their outlines look and what a nice job they did helping to draw the outline of the other children in the class.

   E. *Discussion:* The children will discuss differences in outlines: skirts, pants, lots of hair, short hair, big, little, etc. The children will also discuss how they can use paint or markers to put on different clothes. Motivate or challenge them to put something on the outline that is different and unique. (See activity page.)

   Let them tell what they think is nice about themselves.

6. ***Practice:*** Use a large mirror and have children look at themselves, describe themselves, and tell how they feel about themselves. They may also look in the mirror with a friend and talk about likenesses and differences.

7. ***Independent Use:*** Have children draw a picture of themselves. Compliment them on how good they look, what nice colors they used, what pretty eyes they have, and so on.

8. ***Continuation:*** Have children color the inside of their outline. Take pictures and place them on the board together with their outlines and names. Make a caption such as "It's OK TO BE ME," or something appropriate for the group.

*Suggested Reading* (Acceptance)

Carlson, Nancy. *I Like Me!* New York: Viking Children's Books, 1988.

Lane, Megan Halsey. *Something to Crow About.* New York: Dial Books for Young Readers, 1990.

Lionni, Leo. *Fish Is Fish*. New York: Knopf Books for Young Readers, 1974.

Waber, Bernard. *Ira Sleeps Over*. Boston: Houghton Mifflin, 1975.

Name _____ Date _____

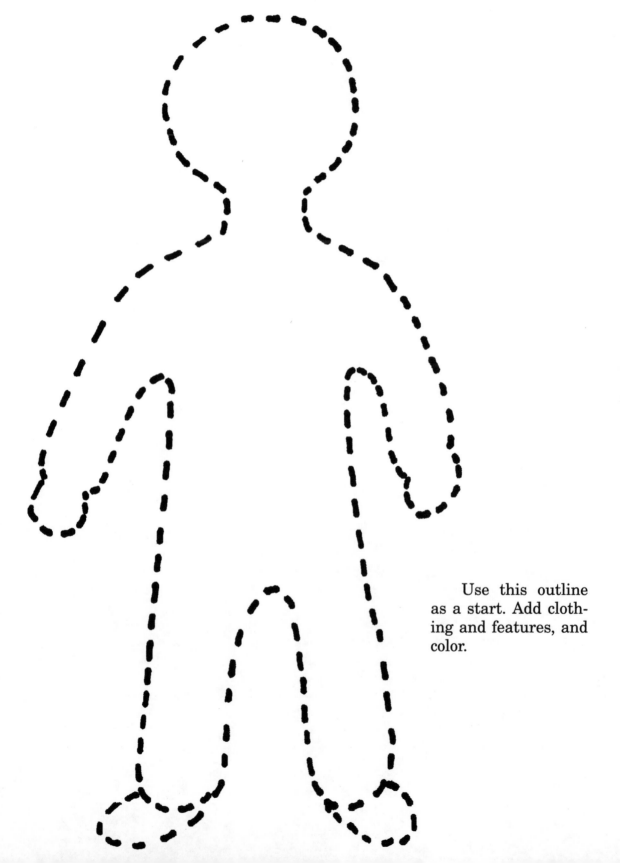

Use this outline as a start. Add clothing and features, and color.

# SOCIAL SKILL

*Expressing Good Things About Oneself*

**Behavioral Objective:** The children will be able to state one thing that they like about themselves.

**Directed Lesson:**

1. **Establish the Need:** The teacher establishes the need for having a positive self-image by stating that it is important to think good thoughts about ourselves because each one of us is special.

2. **Introduction:** The teacher initiates and develops a discussion about liking the way each of us looks and the things that make each person special. During the discussion, the teacher points out something special about each child: the color of hair, a pretty smile, a special characteristic, such as being kind or helpful, good at cleaning up, doing puzzles or building with blocks, etc.

3. **Identify the Skill Components:** (list on board)

   The teacher uses a hand puppet to identify the skill components for the children.

   1. Think about one thing you like about yourself.
   2. Think about one thing you want to say.
   3. Raise your hand to speak.
   4. Wait to be called on to speak.
   5. Look at your classmates and/or teacher, smile, then speak.
   6. Tell what you like by saying "I like myself because . . . "

4. **Model the Skill:** The teacher models the skill steps by saying something nice about him/herself.

5. **Behavioral Rehearsal:**

   A. *Selection:* The teacher selects children to role play.

   B. *Role Play:* The teacher asks the children to think of, choose, then tell one thing they like about themselves. If children have difficulty thinking of something to say, ask for the assistance of classmates in stating something good about them. Or the teacher can express two or three characteristics, and ask the children to choose one that is most appropriate and have them say it.

C. *Completion:* After each role play, reinforce correct behavior, identify inappropriate behaviors, and re-enact role play with corrections. If there are no corrections, role play is complete.

D. *Reinforcers:* Teacher will verbally reinforce the child's statement about self.

E. *Discussion:* Ask students how they feel when they say something nice about themselves. Reinforce positive feelings.

6. **Practice:** The teacher will prepare the appropriate number of copies of the following worksheets—one showing a boy, one a girl—for the class. The heading on the worksheets will be **"I am a very special boy/girl because . . . "**

Each child will be asked to dictate something special about him/herself to complete the sentence, which the teacher will copy on the paper. The children will then color the picture, sign or have their name signed at the top, and the pictures will be displayed.

7. **Independent Use:** Children will be asked to tell about one thing they can do at home that makes them special.

8. **Continuation:** Teacher reminds children, **"If you think good thoughts about yourself, you will make more friends and find it easier to learn new things."** The teacher should continue pointing out the need for this skill as related situations arise.

Name _____   Date _____

<u>I</u> <u>AM</u> <u>A</u> <u>VERY</u> <u>SPECIAL</u> <u>GIRL</u> BECAUSE _____

_____

Name _____  Date _____

<u>I</u> <u>AM</u> <u>A</u> <u>VERY</u> <u>SPECIAL</u> <u>BOY</u> BECAUSE _____

_____

## SOCIAL SKILLS
### *Expressing Our Special Likes and Dislikes*

***Behavioral Objective:*** The children will tell the class about one thing that they enjoy doing.

***Directed Lesson:***

1. ***Establish the Need:*** The teacher establishes the need to understand that there are differences and similarities among people by stating that each of us enjoys many things, and that some of them may be the same and some may be different.

2. ***Introduction:*** The teacher uses a hand puppet, and through the puppet tells the children what the character likes and encourages a discussion of the children's likes and dislikes.

3. ***Identify the Skill Components:*** (List on the board and on a large colorful chart to hang in the room).

   The teacher uses a hand puppet to identify the skill components for the children.

   1. Think about the things that you enjoy.
   2. Choose one thing to share.
   3. Raise a hand to speak.
   4. Wait to be called on.
   5. State whatever it is you enjoy.

4. ***Model the Skill:*** The teacher models the skill by demonstrating the steps involved. Through non-verbal communication, the teacher demonstrates one of the following activities:

   eating

   batting a baseball

   bowling

   reading a book

   The teacher then verbally shares the information.

5. ***Behavioral Rehearsal:***

   A. *Selection:* The teacher will select one child to role play.
   B. *Role Play:* Child will role play by demonstrating each of the skill components related to an activity he/she most enjoys. The role play will be repeated until all children have had a chance to role play.

      C. *Completion:* After each role play, reinforce correct behavior, identify inappropriate behaviors, and re-enact role play with corrections. If there are no corrections, role play is complete.

      D. *Reinforcers:* The teacher uses verbal expressions of admiration and acceptance of each child's contributions.

      E. *Discussion:* After each role play, the children will note what behaviors were included, and those that were left out by responding to the teacher's prompting: e.g., **"Did he/she think of something? Did he/she raise a hand?"**

6. **Practice:** The teacher will distribute to each child a copy of the following worksheet showing four pictures to color. The child will choose a favorite one to share with the group and tell why he/she liked it best.

7. **Independent Use:** Children may cut pictures from magazines and paste them into a book entitled "I Like" and dictate words to be written by the teacher or a student helper from an upper grade.

    They can also be given copies of the Lesson 18 worksheet with owl and mice outlines to color. This relates to three activities children may enjoy—eating, exercising, and reading.

8. **Continuation:** The teacher tells children, **"Remember that each of us has things we like and things we dislike, and that's what makes us different and special from one another."**

Name _____     Date _____

**Name** _____ **Date** _____

eat well    exercise

## SOCIAL SKILL
### *Understanding Our Uniqueness*

**Behavioral Objective:** The children will demonstrate the ability to see themselves as a unique individual by picking out their own silhouette from among those of the class and explaining how they recognize it.

**Directed Lesson:**

1. **Establish the Need:** The teacher refers to previous lessons in which they have all discussed the fact that each child is different from another and that many times each child likes different things. Teacher goes on to point out that each child looks different and that it is very important for children to like and accept the way they look or they will be unhappy.

2. **Introduction:** The teacher will read the following story to the class, or a copy of *The Mixed-Up Chameleon* by Eric Carle (New York: Harper Collins, 1984).

   > **"Here is a story about someone who did not want to be himself and was very unhappy. 'Once there was a little yellow chick who did not want to be himself. He did not want to live in the barnyard and peck in the ground for bugs and corn. At first he tried to be a rooster and stand on the fencepost and crow, but he fell off and bumped his head. Then he tried to be like the horses and drink water from the water trough, but he got water in his nose and choked himself. After that he tried to be like the ducks and swim in the pond. If the farmer's little boy had not come along just at that moment and pulled him out of the water he would have drowned. At last he went to the pig sty and tried to be a pig. He found that he didn't like being covered with mud and rolling in his food the way pigs do. He was so unhappy trying to be some other animal that he went back to the barnyard. He had found out that the best thing for a little yellow chick to be is, a little yellow chick. After that he was very happy for the rest of his life.'"** (Show pictures of farm animals.)

   After they have quietly listened to the story, encourage the children's participation by statements such as **"Wasn't that silly? What a foolish chick (chameleon)!"** Give verbal and non-verbal praise and expressions of approval when the children demonstrate adequate understanding of the moral of the story.

3. **Identify the Skill Components:** (list on board)

   Tell children that they will be following these steps as they learn to pick out their own shadow from others in the class after the teacher traces a silhouette of each child in the class (group).

1. Learn to like yourself as you are.

2. Pick out your own silhouette.

3. Be proud of your features.

4. Point out the best of your features.

5. Learn to know and love each feature.

6. Change what can be changed and you do not like.

7. Be happy with yourself.

**4.   *Model the Skill:*** The teacher will model the skill by first looking among the silhouettes for that of one student, picking it out, and stating why he/she knows it is that of the student to whom it belongs (ex., shape of hair or ponytail, curve of chin, etc.).

**5.   *Behavioral Rehearsal:***

A. *Selection:* The teacher will select several children to choose their own silhouettes from among those in the class.

B. *Role Play:* The children will tell how they know that the one picked is theirs by stating something distinctive about the silhouette. If the children have difficulty stating a distinctive characteristic about their silhouette or cannot find theirs, they should be assisted by another child in finding the silhouette and given some assistance in determining what is special about their silhouette.

C. *Completion:* After each role play, reinforce correct behavior, identify inappropriate behaviors, and re-enact role play with corrections. If there are no corrections, role play is complete.

D. *Reinforcers:* Praise correct behavior verbally.

E. *Discussion:* Why is it important to feel special in some way?

**6.   *Practice:*** Have the children look at the silhouettes of fruits and of animals drawn on the following worksheet pages.

1. The children will point to the silhouette of a fruit and state how they know which fruit it is.

2. The children will point to the silhouette of an animal and state how they know what it is.

3. The children will color both worksheets.

**7.   *Independent Use:*** The children will paste silhouettes of themselves onto a piece of white paper, fold to form a card, print name, and take home to parents.

**8.   *Continuation:*** The teacher will continue to point out the need for each child to like himself or herself as related situations arise.

Name _____    Date _____

Name _____ Date _____

# ZOO ANIMALS

# SHARING

## SOCIAL SKILL
### *Understanding the Need for Sharing with Others*

**Behavioral Objective:** The children will learn to share with other children through games, stories, and toys.

**Directed Lesson:**

1. **Establish the Need:** The teacher establishes the need for sharing by stating the importance of working and/or playing in a group. **"We must take turns and share the toys so that each person has a chance to play."**

2. **Introduction:** The teacher initiates a discussion about the importance of sharing. The teacher might use puppets to explain the word "sharing," and to identify the following skills.

3. **Identify the Skill Components:\*** (list on board)

   1. Think about what you can share.
   2. Choose one thing to share.
   3. Say what you want to share.
   4. Say with whom you want to share.

   **\*NOTE:** When sharing thoughts or ideas in the classroom, two additional Skill Components are necessary:

   1. Raise your hand.
   2. Wait to be called on.

   To illustrate why these two Skill Components are necessary, the teacher will ask the children all to speak at once. This will demonstrate that no one can understand what anyone else has said unless each child waits his or her turn before speaking.

4. **Model the Skill:** The teacher models the skill by giving each child in the group a piece of paper. Then the teacher says: **"We are going to use colored pencils to make a picture. These are the pencils."** (Hold them up.) **"We will all share these pencils."** (Give each child one or two colored pencils.) **"Now we can all make a picture."**

5. **Behavioral Rehearsal:**

   A. *Selection:* All children will role play with a partner. The teacher will tell half of the children to select an activity or game to share with the other half of the group.

B. *Role Play:* The children who select a game or activity will choose a child to share their activity. (Allow them to play about five minutes, then put the activities away.) Now reverse the roles of the children.

C. *Completion:* During and after each role play, reinforce correct behavior, identify inappropriate behavior, and repeat role play if necessary.

D. *Reinforcers:* The teacher will use verbal expressions of acceptance for each child's contributions.

E. *Discussion:* After completion of role play, the teacher will discuss with the children which behaviors were appropriate and which were inappropriate by asking questions such as:

> Did your partner let you play with the toy/game?
>
> Did your partner try to fight with you when you wanted to play with the toy/game?
>
> Did your partner keep the toy/game too long?

6. ***Practice:*** Let the children play games where they must share ("Candyland," "Duck, Duck, Goose"). They may also take turns listening to a recorded story from a tape recorder or take turns sharing toys in small groups.

7. ***Independent Use:*** The children should be encouraged to continue to practice the skill at home by sharing toys and stories or by playing team games with family members and neighbors.

8. ***Continuation:*** The teacher will tell children: **"Using this skill will help you get along better with other children."** The teacher should also continue to point out the need for sharing as related situations arise.

*Suggested Reading*

Hutchins, Pat. *The Doorbell Rang*. New York: Greenwillow, 1986.

Kimmel, Eric. *The Chanukkah Guest*. New York: Holiday, 1990.

Lionni, Leo. *Frederick*. New York: Knopf Books for Young Readers, 1973 (pap.).

The Cheltenham (PA) Elementary School Kindergartners (Author/Illustrator) *We Are All Alike . . . We Are All Different*. New York: Scholastic, 1991.

## SOCIAL SKILL

*Knowing and Accepting the Consequences of Our Actions*

**Behavioral Objective:** The children will know and accept consequences for their own actions.

**Directed Lesson:**

1. **Establish the Need:** The teacher establishes the need by stating the importance of having rules. Rules help us to be safe and happy. When we do not follow the rules, we have to be by ourselves or lose the privilege of playing and learning with our friends and family.

2. **Introduction:** "Today we are going to talk about rules and what happens if you do not do what the rules tell you to do. If you break a rule, you have to take the 'consequences.'

   For example: One of our classroom rules is 'Listen to directions so that you are able to complete your work.' The consequence, or what will happen if you do not listen and do not complete your work, is that you will be left out of a 'special' activity for the day."

---

**Follow All Rules.**

If you don't follow the rules, you are responsible for the consequences:

Consequence #1—Time Out.

Consequence #2—Talk with the teacher.

Consequence #3—Talk with the director or principal.

Consequence #4—Call to parents.

---

The teacher will use hand puppets to identify the following skills.

3. **Identify the Skill Components:** (list on board)

   1. Say what you did wrong.
   2. Say what you should have done.
   3. Say the consequences for what you did.
   4. Accept the consequences without getting upset or angry.

4.   ***Model the Skill:*** The teacher models the skill by demonstrating with hand puppets. Use an inappropriate behavior in the demonstration and the consequences to be received by following the set of four consequences listed in the chart above.

5.   ***Behavioral Rehearsal:***

   A. *Selection:* The teacher selects children to role play in small groups of three or four.

   B. *Role Play:* Students will role play in their small groups some inappropriate behaviors as suggested by the teacher. They will use the skill components to determine and accept the appropriate consequences.

   C. *Completion:* After each role play, reinforce correct behavior, identify inappropriate behaviors, and re-enact role play with corrections.

   D. *Reinforcers:* After the role play, the teacher will give praise for identifying appropriate responses.

   E. The teacher will ask the children: **"How does it feel when we do something wrong and have to take the consequences?"**

6.   ***Practice:*** The teacher will make up situations that the children can act out using the puppets, or flannel board cut-outs.

7.   ***Independent Use:*** Ask children to talk about a consequence for an inappropriate action they did at home and have them draw a picture about this situation. Also have them color copies of the following worksheet, "Wise Old Owl's Classroom Rules and Consequences."

8.   ***Continuation:*** The teacher will tell the children that using this skill every day will make them feel very good.

*Suggested Reading* (Accepting consequences)

Brown, Marcia. *Once a Mouse.* New York: Macmillan Children's Group, 1989 (pap.).

Hutchins, Pat. *Good-Night, Owl!* New York: Macmillan Children's Group, 1972.

Name _____  Date _____

## WISE OLD OWL'S CLASSROOM RULES AND CONSEQUENCES

Ollie Owl says, "Follow the rules." If you do not, then here is the plan.

1. TIME OUT.

2. TALK WITH TEACHER.

3. TALK WITH DIRECTOR OR PRINCIPAL.

4. CALL TO PARENTS.

## SOCIAL SKILL

*Accepting the Consequences for Breaking the Rules*

***Behavioral Objective:*** The children will know and accept the consequences of their actions.

***Directed Lesson:***

1. ***Establish the Need:*** Teacher introduces the idea by initiating a discussion about classroom rules. Ask the children to state some of the rules that exist in their classroom and why. Then, discuss the consequences of not following the rules, asking the children to state some consequences which they feel are appropriate and identify those that exist in their classroom. Discuss the importance of accepting the consequences of their behavior. Point out that when they break a rule, they must accept the consequences, without acting out. Finally, point out that rules are necessary to keep our classroom safe and organized, not to punish children, and that when they break the rules this does not mean they are a bad person.

2. ***Introduction:*** The teacher tells the story of a little boy who broke lots of rules and cried and had tantrums whenever he was asked to sit alone or leave a center. Finally it was decided that this little boy must stay home from school for awhile because he was not grown-up enough to follow rules or accept the consequences and learn to do better when he did not follow the rules.

3. ***Identify the Skill Components:*** (list on board)

   The teacher uses a hand puppet to identify the skill components.

   1. State the rule that you broke.
   2. Learn the correct skill to behave and follow the rule.
   3. Learn what the consequence of breaking the rule is.
   4. Accept the consequence without acting out.

4. ***Model the Skill:*** The teacher models the skill steps, but does not model the inappropriate behavior. Teacher asks the children to assist in modeling by saying, **"Pretend that I have broken a rule. What should I do first?"** Teacher then goes on, with the assistance of the children, and models the four steps that list the skills involved, accepting the consequence without acting out, then verbalizing that they will do better when they remember the rules.

5. ***Behavioral Rehearsal:***

   A. *Selection:* Teacher selects two children to role play.

68

B. *Role Play:* Students select an inappropriate action (e.g., leaving toys on the floor) and role play how to accept the consequences of this action.

C. *Completion:* After each role play, reinforce correct behavior, identify inappropriate behaviors, and re-enact role play with corrections. If there are no corrections, role play is complete.

D. *Reinforcers:* During the role play, the teacher gives praise for and identifies appropriate responses.

E. *Discussion:* How does it feel to be corrected/reprimanded/punished after doing something wrong?

6. ***Practice:*** Teacher will explain that the mouse on the accompanying worksheet got in trouble for eating all the cheese even though it was all the family had for supper. His mother punished him by making him sit in the corner. As you can see, the mouse did not act out when he heard his punishment. He will accept the consequences and sit in the chair. What could the mouse be saying at the top of the page? The students will then be asked to color the picture.

7. ***Independent Use:*** Teacher will initiate a discussion about accepting consequences at home. Teacher will ask the following questions:

   1. Have any of you gotten into trouble at home?

   2. What did you do?

   3. What did you do when you got punished?

   4. What did you learn from this?

8. ***Continuation:*** Teacher tells children, **"If you use this skill whenever you need it, you will be looked at as a 'big person.'"** The need for this skill should be pointed out as related situations arise throughout the year.

Name _____ Date _____

Time Out

## ACCEPTING CONSEQUENCES

## SOCIAL SKILL

*Accepting the Consequences for Our Inappropriate Behavior*

**Behavioral Objective:** The children will know and accept the consequences for their actions.

**Directed Lesson:**

1.  **Establish the Need:** The teacher refers to the previous lesson on accepting consequences and points out to the children that there are other situations besides breaking the rules when they must accept the consequences for inappropriate behavior. Teacher names some other situations such as when a person does not follow directions, or when they do not take part in activities. These are behaviors for which they will need to accept consequences.

2.  **Introduction:** Teacher introduces the story of "The Little Red Hen" and points out that the animals in the story also have to accept consequences that don't come from breaking rules. Read the story of "The Little Red Hen." After the story the teacher discusses the kind of consequences the animals in the story had to accept and encourages them to see that the animals did not break a rule, but they did have to accept the consequences of not participating in the activity.

3.  **Identify the Skill Components:** (list on board)

    Teacher uses a picture of "The Little Red Hen" glued to a tongue depressor to identify the skill components for the children.

    1. Determine what you should have done.
    2. Say what you did wrong.
    3. State the consequence.
    4. Accept the consequence without acting out.

4.  **Model the Skill:** The teacher models the skills involved after presenting imaginary situations in which children at school did not behave desirably or responsibly. For example:

    ◗ a student ran down the hallway and bumped into another person.

    ◗ a student wanted to play with a toy that someone else had, and grabbed it.

    Ask:

    1. What did the student do wrong?

    2. What should the student have done?

71

3. What will happen now?

4. How should the student have behaved?

5. ***Behavioral Rehearsal:***

   A. *Selection:* The teacher selects four participants for role playing.

   B. *Role Play:* Each acts out the character from the story "Little Red Hen." Role play each animal's behavior.

   C. *Completion:* After each role play, reinforce correct behavior, identify inappropriate behaviors, and reenact role play with corrections. If there are no corrections, role play is complete.

   D. *Reinforcers:* The teacher gives praise for those responses that indicate understanding of the skill.

   E. *Discussion:* What do the children consider a fair punishment for each animal's behavior?

6. ***Practice:*** The children have a coloring sheet of the characters from the story of "The Little Red Hen." Teacher may review the story "The Little Red Hen." Ask what the consequence was for each animal's behavior. Ask what each one will do differently the next time. Teacher then tells children to color the worksheet.

7. ***Independent Use:*** Ask children to talk about a personal experience with consequences (in the school setting, home setting, etc.).

8. ***Continuation:*** Teacher tells children, **"It is important for each one of us to treat other people the way we want them to treat us."**

Name _____     Date _____

## SOCIAL SKILL

*Remembering to Walk—Not Run—in the Classroom*

**Behavioral Objective:** The children will demonstrate self-control by remembering to walk instead of run in the classroom.

**Directed Lesson:**

1.  **Establish the Need:** The teacher states briefly to the children how walking instead of running in the classroom keeps the people in the class from being hurt and from hurting others.

2.  **Introduction:** The teacher uses a large picture of a child who is crying and asks the children to tell what they think could have happened when this child ran indoors, and how the tears could have been prevented.

    The teacher will use hand puppets to identify the following skills.

3.  **Identify the Skill Components:** (list on board)

    1. Stop and look before moving around.
    2. Walk slowly and carefully when moving from place to place.
    3. Remind others to walk and not run.

4.  **Model the Skill:** The teacher models the skill by demonstrating the act of calmly walking and carefully moving around objects.

5.  **Behavioral Rehearsal:**

    A. *Selection:* Set up an "obstacle course" with several chairs. Select one child to walk through the "obstacle course" first.
    B. *Role Play:* The teacher will remove the chairs and substitute them with children to form an "obstacle course" pattern. The child chosen to go first will walk through the obstacle course without touching any of the other children.

    This game can be continued until every child has had a chance to walk through the obstacle course.
    C. *Completion:* Restate and affirm correct behavior. Give each child a sticker for obeying the good working rules.
    D. *Reinforcers:* Verbal praise and non-verbal praise should continually be given to those children who practice self-control and maintain their correct behavior.

E. *Discussion:* The teacher will ask the children: **"What might have happened if you had run through the obstacle course instead of walked?"** After the children have responded, the teacher may also ask the children **"Where else is it important to always walk slowly?"** (In the hall, in the lunchroom, in a store, in your home. You *walk* indoors. Outdoors you can *walk* and *run* when appropriate.)

6. ***Practice:*** Children can use blocks stacked as obstacles to discover how slowly they have to walk in order to not knock down or touch any of the blocks. Have the children move the blocks closer together after each attempt.

7. ***Independent Use:*** The children are asked to observe, wherever they are, the object or people around them so as not to run into them.

8. ***Continuation:*** Give daily recognition and affirmation to children practicing self-control by observing the objects and people around them and being careful not to get hurt or to hurt others by getting too close.

*Suggested Reading*

Aliki. *We Are Best Friends.* New York: Morrow, 1987 (pap.)

McGovern, Ann. *Too Much Noise.* Boston: Houghton Mifflin, 1967, 1992 (pap.)

Wells, Rosemary. *Unfortunately Harriett.* New York: Dial Books for Young Readers, 1972.

## SOCIAL SKILL

*Remembering to Walk—Not Run—in School*

**Behavioral Objective:** The child will demonstrate self-control by walking slowly when going from one area of the classroom to another or from one part of the building to another.

**Directed Lesson:**

1. **Establish the Need:** Teacher initiates a discussion of the importance of safety when walking from place to place, in and out of the classroom.

2. **Introduction:** The teacher will use a picture of a little girl sitting on the table having her legs bandaged. She asks the children to tell what they think could have happened to the little girl and how she could have prevented it. After the discussion the teacher emphasizes the importance of walking instead of running and expresses an expectation that the children will be able to demonstrate good self-control by walking in and out of the classroom at a slow rate of speed.

3. **Identify the Skill Components:** (list on board)

   Teacher uses a hand puppet to identify for the children the skills involved in practicing self-control by walking carefully and slowly.

   1. Stop and think before moving around, especially outside the classroom.
   2. Walk slowly when moving from place to place.
   3. When reminded, slow down and walk carefully.

4. **Model the Skill:** Teacher models the skill by moving from place to place in the room while children observe the slow rate of speed. While walking, teacher points out the objects that they could bump into or fall over if running, but does not actually demonstrate the undesirable behavior.

5. **Behavioral Rehearsal:**

   A. *Selection:* Teacher asks half of the class to participate in the role play.
   B. *Role Play:* After placing chairs around the room as obstacles, the teacher instructs the children to move around the room and demonstrate self-control by walking in a safe manner. Then, the other half of the group should be allowed to role play. During this time, a background recording of slow, soothing music can be played.

      C. *Completion:* After each role play, reinforce correct behavior, identify inappropriate behaviors, and reenact role play with corrections. If there are no corrections, role play is complete.

      D. *Reinforcers:* During the role plays the teacher will use verbal and non-verbal rewards and expressions of praise to provide reinforcement to the children.

      Praise and appreciation, when the children demonstrate their mastery of self-control, should be expressed often during the school year to maintain the skill.

      E. *Discussion:* The teacher can discuss with the class the manner in which the children walked and allow the children to point out any undesirable behaviors.

6. **Practice:** The children are taken to the hallway. Some are instructed to go slowly in one direction, while others are instructed to go slowly in another direction. They are asked to walk to a certain point and return by walking slowly and carefully.

7. **Independent Use:** A ticket system can be implemented. Children will receive "traffic tickets" for speed violation.

      first ticket—Time Out

      second ticket—loss of a privilege

      third ticket—a note that goes home

Each day, the slate is wiped clean and the ticket system is back in operation. At the end of the week, those with no traffic violations can have five extra minutes of play time and receive the accompanying "Good Sport" Award, which they are permitted to take home, while the speeders catch up on their rest (heads down).

8. **Continuation:** The teacher points out the need for exercising self-control whenever related situations arise.

# GOOD SPORT AWARD

To:
_____

For:
_____
_____
_____
_____

# SOCIAL SKILLS
## *Using a Moderate Tone of Voice*

***Behavioral Objective:*** The children will demonstrate self-control by using a moderate tone of voice when addressing classmates and the teacher.

***Directed Lesson:***

1.  ***Establish the Need:*** Teacher initiates a discussion about the appropriate voice level in the classroom.

2.  ***Introduction:*** Play a tape recording or a record at a loud and uncomfortable level. Ask the children to respond to this by expressing how they felt about listening to something so loud. Teacher will stress those responses which point out that it is uncomfortable to work and play in an environment which is too noisy and will then state the expectation that the children will be able to practice self-control and talk with quiet "indoor" voices.

3.  ***Identify the Skill Components:*** (list on board)

    The teacher uses a very quiet, whispering hand puppet to identify the skill components for the children.

    > 1. Stop and think before talking.
    > 2. Use a quiet voice when speaking.
    > 3. Quiet down when you see the "shh" sign.
    > 4. Help others to use a quiet voice.

4.  ***Model the Skill:*** Teacher models the appropriate behavior by having a quiet conversation with the hand puppet. **"Hello, what is your name? Would you like to play today?"** Puppet responds in an appropriate voice, **"My name is . . . Yes, I'd like to play."** Teacher says **"I like the way you speak. You use a nice 'indoor' voice. I can hear you and it doesn't hurt my ears."**

5.  ***Behavioral Rehearsal:***

    A. Selection: Teacher selects half the class to participate in the role play.

    B. *Role Play:* Using a familiar nursery rhyme or fingerplay, the teacher asks the selected children to recite the verse in their loudest voices. The students are to stop role playing when the teacher demonstrates the "shh" sign. She then asks the audience to respond to the loudness of the selected group's voices. Using verbal and non-verbal cues, she encourages appropriate responses and then selects the other half of the class to perform the rhyme or fingerplay in normal "indoor" voices. She asks the group that is listening to respond to them.

    C. *Completion:* After each role play, reinforce correct behavior, identify inappropriate behaviors, and reenact role play with corrections. If there are no corrections, role play is complete.

    D. *Reinforcers:* During the role play, the teacher will use verbal and non-verbal praise and expressions of approval to develop the children's understanding and elicit appropriate responses. In order to maintain the appropriate behavior, the teacher should remember to regularly praise and express appreciation to the class for practicing self-control by using soft voices.

    E. *Discussion:* The teacher emphasizes that responses which are more pleasant and easier to listen to are those which are said in a quiet tone of voice.

6.   *Practice:* Every day one child may be responsible for listening for loud voices. That child will gently touch the shoulder of the child talking loudly and point to a sign that says "SHH!"

7.   *Independent Use:* The children will be given the following "SHH" coloring sheet which they will complete to the best of their ability, take home and ask their parents to sign after the child has explained to them the social skill. All children who can explain the skill to an adult or older child at school may receive a reward (sticker, stamp, and so on).

8.   *Continuation:* Whenever related situations arise, the teacher reminds children to please use a quiet voice. Signals can serve as reminders, such as turning out the lights, playing chords on a piano, tapping a drum, and so on.

Name _____ Date _____

# SOCIAL SKILL

*Choosing a Peaceful Approach to Problem Solving*

**Behavioral Objective:** The child will be able to choose, with adult assistance, a peaceful approach to solving a problem.

**Directed Lesson:**

1. **Establish the Need:** Building problem-solving skills fosters independence, builds self-confidence and helps reduce conflicts.

2. **Introduction:** The teacher will tell the following story to the children.

   > **"Johnny and Bobby were playing with cars in the block corner. Johnny had the red car first. Bobby came and grabbed it. Johnny hit him hard and Bobby ran screaming to the teacher."**

   Discuss the story with the children, helping them to state the problem and offer alternative ways of solving it.

   The teacher will use hand puppets to identify the following skills.

3. **Identify the Skill Components:** (list on board)
   1. State the problem.
   2. Talk about the problem.
   3. Tell each other what you think would solve the problem.
   4. Find a solution both of you can agree on.
   5. If no solution can be agreed upon, ask the teacher to help solve the problem.

4. **Model the Skill:** The teacher models the skill using the hand puppets to dramatize a peaceful approach to solving the problem stated above in the introduction.

5. **Behavioral Rehearsal:**
   A. *Selection:* The teacher selects four pairs of children to role play solving different problems in a peaceful manner.
   B. *Role Play:* Have children work in pairs to solve constructive problems. One pair will demonstrate how to use a water fountain when two want a drink simultaneously.

Another pair will learn how to assemble a picture puzzle. Other pairs of children can solve various conflict problems. One conflict might be "who picked the toy first" and sharing the toy might be the solution. Another conflict might occur when two children want to sit in the same place. The solution might be to take turns.

C. *Completion:* After each role play, reinforce correct behavior and identify inappropriate behavior. Re-enact role play with corrections. If there are no corrections, role play is complete.

D. *Reinforcers:* Verbally praise the "actors."

E. *Discussion:* Ask children if there are other problems that come up, and talk about how they can be solved peacefully.

6. ***Practice:*** Offer daily reinforcement of problem-solving skills especially in a peaceful way. Children who do not fight for two weeks but solve their conflicts (problems) peacefully will receive copies of the following worksheet, "I'm A Problem Solver!" They will color it and are permitted to take it home.

7. ***Independent Use:*** The use of skills to solve problems in a peaceful manner can be identified and reinforced in all activities (e.g., outdoor play, home, etc.).

8. ***Continuation:*** The teacher will recognize and affirm behaviors when solving problems peacefully, wherever they occur, on a daily basis.

Name _____ Date _____

## I'M A PROBLEM SOLVER!

## SOCIAL SKILL
### *Solving a Problem by Talking*

**Behavioral Objective:** Children will demonstrate the ability to solve a conflict not by fighting but by talking to the person with whom they are involved or by asking the teacher to help settle the conflict.

**Directed Lesson:**

1.  **Establish the Need:** The teacher comments that when we are working we must learn to work together and solve problems peacefully or we will not have a safe and peaceful place to work and play.

2.  **Introduction:** Teacher tells of a situation where two children wanted to work with the same puzzle and neither one would give it up. Soon the children were pushing and shouting at each other and finally one of them got hurt and began to cry. Teacher asks the children to discuss how the children could have settled this problem and be kept from getting hurt.

3.  **Identify the Skill Components:** (list on board)

    The teacher uses a hand puppet to identify the skill components for the children.

    1. When a problem arises, use your words and not your body (hands or feet).
    2. Talk about the problem to the other person.
    3. Ask for help if you cannot settle the problem.
    4. Agree that the problem is settled.
    5. Shake hands.

4.  **Model the Skill:** The teacher uses two hand puppets to demonstrate the correct problem-solving strategy. The puppets have a conflict over an activity and use the skill components to settle their conflict.

5.  **Behavioral Rehearsal:**

    A. *Selection:* The teacher selects four to five children to participate in the role play.
    B. *Role Play:* Two children are asked to pretend to have a conflict about who can play with a particular toy. The other children are asked to help settle the dispute by telling the disputants what actions to take in order to settle the conflict in a peaceful manner.

85

    C. *Completion:* After each role play, reinforce correct behavior, identify inappropriate behaviors, and reenact role play with corrections. If there are no corrections, role play is complete.

    D. *Reinforcers:* Reinforcement is given for sharing and using only words to settle the conflict. Use verbal praise and/or a star cut-out of paper for the "problem solvers."

    E. *Discussion:* Children will discuss why it is important to solve a conflict by using words instead of physical actions.

6. **Practice:** The teacher sets out several favorite games and activities. The children and teacher review the alternatives to conflict: sharing, going to another center, taking turns, or choosing some other game or activity. Three children are then asked to choose an activity and use the skill steps to avoid conflict when two children select the same activity.

7. **Independent Use:** Children will tell how they settle a conflict they have with other members of their family when they use their words.

8. **Continuation:** The teacher continually points out the need for this skill as related situations arise.

## SOCIAL SKILL

*Completing a Task and Putting Away Materials*

**Behavioral Objective:** The children will choose a short activity. After completion of the activity, the children will return the material which was used for the activity to its proper location.

**Directed Lesson:**

1. **Establish the Need:** The teacher stresses the importance of being good workers and learners. The teacher will explain that a child is a good worker when he/she learns something from his/her work. A child is also a good worker when he/she completes a task and puts the materials away properly.

2. **Introduction:** The teacher chooses an activity and starts it. The teacher pretends to be frustrated and sloppily puts the materials back anywhere except in the correct location. Then he/she asks the children: **"Did I learn anything by doing that activity?"** The teacher explains to the children that if they do not understand the activity, they might become upset. When that happens, the best thing to do is to ask the teacher or a parent for help.

   The teacher will use hand puppets to identify the following skills.

3. **Identify the Skill Components:** (list on board)

   1. Choose an activity.
   2. Complete the activity.
   3. Ask questions if you do not understand.
   4. Return the activity as neatly as you found it and to the same location.

4. **Model the Skill:** The teacher models the skill by choosing, completing, and putting away an activity.

5. **Behavioral Rehearsal:**

   A. *Selection:* The teacher selects five children to role play.
   B. *Role Play:* The children will choose an activity and bring it to the center of the circle. The children will complete the activity. If the children do not know how to complete the activity, they will ask questions and get assistance from the teacher. The children will briefly explain about their activity while they are working on it. They will return the activity to the appropriate location after it has been completed.

    C. *Completion:* Reinforce correct behaviors and identify inappropriate behaviors. Re-enact role play with corrections if necessary.

    D. *Reinforcers:* Use verbal praise and non-verbal praise (pat on the back, hug, smile) for "actors."

    E. *Discussion:* Discuss with the children individually when they put an activity away whether they have put it away correctly or incorrectly. Also discuss the need for completing an activity.

6. **Practice:** Give children daily practice in completing a task and returning the materials used to do the activity to the appropriate location.

7. **Independent Use:** Send a note home explaining this Social Skill. Ask parents to monitor their child's work and play and to encourage their child to complete any task and to put all parts back in the correct place when finished.

8. **Continuation:** Remind children of this skill and the necessity of this skill as related situations arise. Reinforce children who complete their work and put their materials away in the appropriate location.

# SOCIAL SKILL
## *Finishing Each Activity That Is Started*

**Behavioral Objective:** The children will choose (or be assigned) an activity, take it to the appropriate area, complete the activity and return it to its proper location before they choose another.

**Directed Lesson:**

1. **Establish the Need:** In large group discussion the teacher discusses the importance of being "good workers and learners" and points out that students are good workers when they finish whatever job has been chosen or assigned and, upon finishing this work, carefully put all materials away.

2. **Introduction:** Teacher may tell a short story about a little child who is not happy and does not learn. Why? Because the child always complains about not being able to do puzzles or build buildings or fix patterns. The teacher points out to the children that this little child can't learn to do things because there is no attempt made to finish what is started. In order to learn, we must all complete one activity before going to another.

3. **Identify the Skill Components:** (list on board)

   The teacher uses hand puppets to identify for the children the components of this skill.

   1. Choose or accept an activity.
   2. Take the activity to an appropriate location.
   3. Complete activity as best you can.
   4. Return activity to its proper location.

4. **Model the Skill:** Teacher models the skill by choosing, completing and putting away an activity.

5. **Behavioral Rehearsal:**
   A. *Selection:* Teacher selects children to role play. Choose several children who can give an effective demonstration.
   B. *Role Play:* Have the children select short activities, bring them to the center of the group and complete the activities. Then, have them put them away.
   C. *Completion:* After each role play, reinforce correct behavior, identify inappropriate behaviors, and reenact role play with corrections. If there are no corrections, role play is complete.

    D. *Reinforcers:* Verbal and non-verbal praise and expressions of approval. Children will be instructed to point out and give praise to their classmates who complete activities.

    E. *Discussion:* Why is it important to finish what you start?

6. ***Practice:*** Give a short assignment. Have children complete it and check it over together and return it to its proper place.

7. ***Independent Use:*** Children will be given a short note such as the following to take home explaining to parents that they are working on the social skill of completing assignments. The parent will be asked to give the child a short job to do and when the job is done the parent will sign his/her name in the appropriate place. Children will receive a small reward for returning the note.

An alternative to this is to create an in-class system for minor jobs. Children can be given recognition for satisfactory completion of each job.

8. ***Continuation:*** Teacher will remind children that good workers and learners finish the jobs they begin as related situations arise. In order to learn, we must complete one activity before going on to another.

Date: _____

Dear Family:

In school I am learning to finish work that I choose to do or that my teacher assigns to me.

Will you help me at home? Please give me a small job to do. Here are some suggestions:

1. Putting away the dishes.

2. Helping to put away groceries.

3. Hanging up clothes.

I will do my best to finish what you give me to do. When I finish, please sign this note so that I can return it to my teacher. Thank you!

Child: _____

Parent Signature: _____ Date: _____

## SOCIAL SKILL

### *Responding Constructively to Name Calling*

**Behavioral Objective:** With the assistance of adults, children will be able to demonstrate that they can deal with name calling by ignoring the action or verbally expressing to the name caller their dislike of that behavior.

**Directed Lesson:**

1. **Establish the Need:** The teacher establishes the need for learning to deal with name calling by discussing with the children the hurt caused by name calling, pointing out that sometimes some of the children will forget the rule that we call each person by his or her given name.

2. **Introduction:** The teacher tells the following story:

   **"Once upon a time, there was a little bunny named Joe who had great big floppy ears. All the other little bunnies had neat pointed ears and they teased their brother and called him 'Flop-Flop'! Joe bunny would cry and hide in the bushes. One day when he was hiding from all the other bunnies who had been calling him names, he lifted up his large floppy ears and found that he could hear sounds from far away in the forest. He could hear sounds that the other bunnies, with their small neat ears, could not hear. He heard the sound of a hunter walking through the forest to catch some bunnies to make a rabbit stew! Joe ran to tell the other bunnies because they had not heard the hunter's footsteps. Just in time, they jumped into their bunny holes and escaped from the hunter! Joe bunny was very proud of himself for saving his family. He told the other bunnies that if they ever called him names again, he would tell them he did not like to be called bad names and then he would ignore them and not listen."**

   The teacher uses hand puppets to identify the following skills to use when someone calls you a name.

3. **Identify the Skill Components:** (list on board)

   1. Ask the person to stop name calling.
   2. Look the person in the eye and say, "My name is _____."
   3. Explain that name calling hurts and is inappropriate.
   4. Ignore the person who does not stop name calling.
   5. Walk away.

4.  ***Model the Skill:*** The teacher will model the skill by using two hand puppets. The teacher will demonstrate the act of name calling with one puppet and use the other puppet to demonstrate the skills used in dealing with name calling.

5.  ***Behavioral Rehearsal:***

    A. *Selection:* The teacher selects two children to role play.

    B. *Role Play:* The teacher assigns roles. One child will be instructed to call the other child "Flop Flop." The other child will use the skill components to react to the name calling. (See story in Introduction section.)

    C. *Completion:* Praise the behavior that deals with name calling and correct the way to handle it, if necessary.

    D. *Reinforcers:* Verbal praise for the "actors."

    E. *Discussion:* Additional verbal reinforcement. Discuss with all the children how they can react to name calling.

6.  ***Practice:*** Let each child select a partner. As the teacher calls each child's name, the child responds by saying one complimentary thing about his or her partner.

7.  ***Independent Use:*** The teacher will tell the children that they can deal with name calling anywhere—but they may need an adult to help them. If there is not an adult to help, then they should walk away from the person who is calling them names.

8.  ***Continuation:*** Assist children in dealing with name calling by providing them with skills to use. Encourage them when they attempt to use the skills by verbally affirming their efforts.

*Suggested Reading*

Bonsall, Crosby. *It's Mine! A Greedy Book.* New York: Harper Collins Children's Books, 1964.

Wells, Rosemary. *Benjamin and Tulip.* New York: Dial Books for Young Readers, 1977.

Yashima, Taro. *Crow Boy.* New York: Viking Children's Books, 1955, 1976 (pap. Puffin Books).

## SOCIAL SKILL
### Communicating Anger Using Words

**Behavioral Objective:** The children will communicate their anger by using words to express how they are feeling, such as "I am angry."

**Directed Lesson:**

1.  **Establish the Need:** Children need to learn to communicate their needs and feelings so they can be guided and assisted.

2.  **Introduction:** The teacher will tell the following story:

    **"One day at our school _____, we were busy working in our centers. Larry and Diana were in the doll corner and Larry was dressing the big doll. Diana tried to grab it and Larry wouldn't give it to her. Diana became angry and spit on Larry and kicked him. Larry screamed and cried and the teacher closed the doll corner so they could discuss what happened."**

    The teacher discusses the situation with the children and talks about the desired behaviors.

    The teacher will use hand puppets to identify the following skills.

3.  **Identify the Skill Components:** (list on board)

    1. Say to each other "I am angry."
    2. Tell each other why you are angry.
    3. Tell each other what he/she did that made you angry.
    4. Tell each other that you will not do it again.
    5. Shake hands and be friends again.
    6. Ask an adult to help if you cannot agree.

4.  **Model the Skill:** The teacher will use two hand puppets to model the situation from the story.

5.  **Behavioral Rehearsal:**

    A. *Selection:* The teacher selects two children to role play with the puppets or by themselves.

    B. *Role Play:* The children will be assigned and will carry out roles with assistance. Role plays could include: stepping out of line, trying to be the first to the water fountain, grabbing food, fighting, kicking, spitting, etc.

C. *Completion:* Reinforce correct behavior, identify inappropriate behavior, and re-enact role play if necessary. If there are no corrections, role play is complete.

D. *Reinforcers:* Verbal praise for the "actors."

E. *Discussion:* The teacher will ask all children to tell what they will do if someone makes them angry.

6. *Practice:* When children are angry, they can be given a blank sheet of paper and told to **"Draw an angry picture that shows how they are feeling."** Playdough can also be used to work out and talk about angry feelings.

7. *Independent Use:* The teacher should make sure that the skills are identified and reinforced throughout the year.

8. *Continuation:* Daily recognition and affirmation for children who demonstrate by their behavior that they are learning how to deal with anger in a peaceful way.

*Suggested Reading*

Burningham, John. *Borka: The Adventures of a Goose with No Feathers.* Topsfield, MA: Salem House Pubs., 1981.

Carle, Eric. *The Grouchy Ladybug.* New York: Harper Collins Children's Books, 1977, 1986 (pap.).

Zion, Gene. *The Meanest Squirrel I Ever Met.* New York: Macmillan, 1982.

# SOCIAL SKILL
## *Learning to Avoid Tattling*

***Behavioral Objective:*** The children will learn to avoid tattling when inappropriate.

***Directed Lesson:***

1. ***Establish the Need:*** Unnecessary tattling is a distraction to others. A child who tattles too often may become disliked by other children. When someone is doing something dangerous, only then is it important to tell an adult.

2. ***Introduction:*** The teacher will ask the children: **"How do you feel when someone tattles on you"?** During the discussion of the children's responses, the teacher may want to give a response to the question also.

   The teacher will use hand puppets to identify the following skills.

3. ***Identify the Skill Components:*** (list on board)

   1. Look at what another person is doing.
   2. Decide if it is safe or unsafe.
   3. Continue with your own activity if the other person's action is safe.
   4. Do not tell anybody about it.
   5. Tell an adult if the other person's action is dangerous, and/or unsafe.

4. ***Model the Skill:*** The teacher demonstrates being a tattler. Present an example of a minor (safe) and major (unsafe) disturbance.

5. ***Behavioral Rehearsal:***

   A. *Selection:* Choose three children and assign two of them to different activities (i.e.: one to the puzzle table, and one to the manipulatives). Assign the remaining child to be the teacher.

   B. *Role Play:* Assign one child to be the "Tattler" and instruct him/her to go to the "Teacher" and tattle about something minor or major that the other child is doing. Assist the "Teacher" in asking questions which determine if it is appropriate for the "Tattler" to report the behavior of the other child. Questions the "Teacher" can ask may include:

   **"Is he/she going to be hurt?"**

**"Is he/she doing good work in our classroom?"**

Help the "Teacher" to determine if it was really necessary to report the other child's activity or if it was just tattling.

    C. *Completion:* Reinforce the positive aspects of the role play.

    D. *Reinforcers:* Compliment the "actors."

    E. *Discussion:* Review when it is appropriate to tell an adult what someone else is doing, and when it is appropriate to say nothing.

**Practice:** The teacher will give praise to the class about how well they worked today without occurrence of tattling.

**Independent Use:** Encourage the children to be helpful to their parents by carrying over this behavior at home.

**Continuation:** Give daily reinforcement of positive behavior. Impress upon the children that if they are all doing what they are supposed to be doing there is never any need to "tattle."

*Suggested Reading*

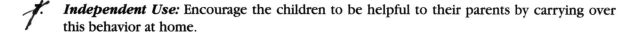

Cohen, Miriam. *Will I Have a Friend?* New York: Macmillan Children's Books, 1967, 1989 (pap.).

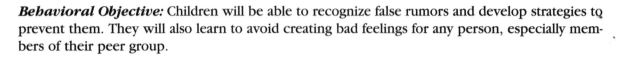

## SOCIAL SKILL
### *Stopping False Rumors*

**Behavioral Objective:** Children will be able to recognize false rumors and develop strategies to prevent them. They will also learn to avoid creating bad feelings for any person, especially members of their peer group.

**Directed Lesson:**

1. **Establish the Need:** The purposes are to console the person who is damaged by a false rumor, to stop the rumor, and to recognize that a rumor is not factual.

2. **Introduction:** The teacher gives examples of a false rumor.

   The teacher leads a discussion with the class about what happens when the teacher/children are constantly disturbed by tattling during their lessons. How can we prevent this?

   Teacher explains that there are some interruptions that are necessary (important). Teacher identifies necessary interruptions.

3. **Identify the Skill Components:** (list on board or sentence strips)

   1. Work quietly at centers.
   2. Share games and activities.
   3. Tell the teacher only important things (facts) about another child and not rumors.
   4. Interrupt the teacher only when it is necessary.

4. **Model the Skill:** Teacher gives examples of necessary interruptions using a hand puppet. Children discuss what kind of interruptions are important when they report on the actions of another child.

5. **Behavioral Rehearsal:**

   A. *Selection:* Teacher arranges groups of five to role play. One child acts as teacher, four as children.

   B. *Role Play:* "Teacher" works with three children in a center and the fourth student tattles about behavior of another child to the "teacher." Repeat several times to demonstrate tattling that is unnecessary, and tattling that is false.

   C. *Completion:* After each role play, reinforce correct behavior, identify inappropriate behaviors and re-enact role play with corrections. If there are no corrections, role play is complete.

    D. *Reinforcers:* During the role play, the teacher will use verbal praise and non-verbal rewards. Group reinforcement should be expressed at the end of a day or session.

    E. *Discussion:* How did the participants in the role play feel? Should they have informed the teacher each time or not?

6. **Practice:** The teacher will discuss that the two-way telephone should be used only for important information and not to spread false rumors or for tattling.

7. **Independent Use:** The children will be given the accompanying worksheet to color to the best of their ability. They will take it home and ask an adult at home to sign it, after the child has explained the Social Skill they have learned in school today.

8. **Continuation:** The teacher tells the children, **"If you use this skill whenever and wherever you need it, you will learn much more and become a better student."** Teachers should continue pointing out the need for this skill as related situations arise.

Name _____ Date _____

## SOCIAL SKILL
### *Understanding and Accepting Change*

**Behavioral Objective:** The children will learn to understand and to accept change. The children will also learn that change is unavoidable.

**Directed Lesson:**

1. **Establish the Need:** Change is often difficult to accept, but in life, change is unavoidable. Change can make you happy or it can make you sad. Many times it is necessary to accept changes and learn that they make you grow.

2. **Introduction:** The teacher will tell the following story.

> **"The Pre-Kindergarten class at _____ had a field trip planned for Friday. They were going to the park for a picnic. All the boys and girls were very excited. On Friday, the bus arrived and all the children got on the bus. As the bus got closer to the park, it began to rain hard. The children arrived at the park and walked in the rain. Sooner than they had planned, the children got back on the bus and returned to school."**

The teacher will use hand puppets to identify the following skills.

3. **Identify the Skill Components:** (list on board)

    1. Realize and acknowledge changes cheerfully.
    2. Make a change an adventure.
    3. Make the best out of each change.

4. **Model the Skill:** The teacher models the skill by promising the children they will be going outside to play jump rope. The teacher then realizes that there is no jump rope. The children will observe the reaction of the teacher, who accepts the change cheerfully. Questions are asked to involve the children in the modeling of the skill.

| | |
|---|---|
| **"What will happen now?"** | (Think of other choices.) |
| **"What could we do instead?"** | (Play ball. Skip. Hop on one foot.) |
| **"How should I act?"** | (Glad to be able to play, even though it's not the game I was planning on.) |

**5.**   ***Behavioral Rehearsal:***

   A. *Selection:* The teacher selects a small group of children to role play.

   B. *Role Play:* One child acts as the teacher, the others as the students. They will act out in the role play how they will react to a park trip disappointment (from the story in the Introduction and the information in the Model the Skill section).

   C. *Completion:* Restate and affirm appropriate reactions to and acceptance of the change as found in the role play.

   D. *Reinforcers:* Verbally praise the "actors."

   E. *Discussion:* The teacher will tell the children that many times, a change can be for the better. The teacher will ask the children to give examples.

**6.**   ***Practice:*** The teacher will tell the children that one regular routine for the day will be changed. At the end of the day, the children will tell how they accepted the change.

**7.**   ***Independent Use:*** The teacher initiates a discussion about accepting change at home, citing examples such as moving and making new friends.

**8.**   ***Continuation:*** The teacher will tell the children that changes make our lives more exciting and we need to accept them. The teacher will ask children to think of changes that have made our lives better, e.g., telephone, computers, appliances and other changes that are more difficult to accept. Reinforce the concept throughout the school year when unavoidable changes occur in the class routine or at home.

*Suggested Reading*

DeRegniers, Beatrice Schenk. *May I Bring a Friend?* New York: Macmillan Children's Group, 1989.

Greenfield, Eloise. *She Come Bringing Me That Little Baby Girl.* New York: Harper Collins Children's Books, 1990.

Greenwood, Pamela. *What About My Goldfish?* Boston: Houghton Mifflin (Clarion), 1993.

## SOCIAL SKILL

*Accepting and Adjusting to Change*

**Behavioral Objective:** The children will learn to be able to understand and accept change. The children will also learn that change is unavoidable.

**Directed Lesson:**

1.  **Establish the Need:** Change is often difficult to accept but is unavoidable in life. Reaction to change can make us either happy or sad. It is necessary to accept changes that make us sad and to learn to create better conditions in the future to ensure happiness.

2.  **Introduction:** The teacher says, **"Today, boys and girls, I am going to tell you a story about a Kindergarten class. They did not get to go on a field trip that they had been planning for all year. They planned and they planned to go to the zoo. Everyone was so excited because today was the day and they could hardly wait for the bus to come and take them. The teacher was called to the office and was told that the bus broke down and there was no other way to get to the zoo. The teacher told the class that the zoo trip was cancelled and discussed what they would do in place of the trip."**

    Teacher discusses with the class alternative activities for the zoo trip.

3.  **Identify the Skill Components:** (list on board or sentence strips)

    1. Accept that things cannot always turn out the way they are planned.
    2. Choose or accept an alternate activity.
    3. Be ready to adjust to changes gracefully.

4.  **Model the Skill:** Teacher pretends to receive a note from the office stating that the assembly program for the day has been cancelled. Teacher than talks through the three skill components listed.

5.  **Behavioral Rehearsal:**

    A. *Selection:* The teacher selects several participants to role play.
    B. *Role Play:* One child acts as the teacher, the others as the students. They will then re-enact the zoo trip story with positive outcomes.
    C. *Completion:* After each role play, reinforce correct behavior, identify inappropriate behaviors and re-enact role play with corrections. If there are no corrections, role play is complete.

      D. *Reinforcers:* The teacher should give verbal and non-verbal praise and expressions of approval for those responses that indicate understanding of the skill.

      E. *Discussion:* The teacher can discuss with the class the manner in which the children can accept change and have students cite examples for these changes.

6. **Practice:** The teacher will tell the children that today they will change one daily routine. Children will provide feedback on how they accepted and adjusted to the change.

7. **Independent Use:** The teacher initiates a discussion about accepting change at home. The children will color and take home a copy of the following worksheet. Encourage them to explain the Social Skill which was learned as school.

8. **Continuation:** Teacher tells the children, **"If you use this skill whenever and wherever you need it, you will become a happier person and a better student."** Teacher should continue pointing out this skill as related situations arise.

Name _____ Date _____

# SOCIAL SKILL

## *Discriminating Between Happy and Sad Feelings*

***Behavioral Objective:*** The children will learn to discriminate between happy and sad feelings by showing the correct side of the happy/sad hand puppet when asked a question about a situation.

***Directed Lesson:***

1. ***Establish the Need:*** The teacher establishes the need by asking the children to give examples of things that make them happy and things that make them sad. The teacher stresses the importance of understanding feelings and knowing when they and others are happy or sad.

2. ***Introduction:*** The teacher introduces the story *The Three Little Pigs*. The teacher tells the children to listen carefully and try to remember when the pigs are happy and when the pigs are sad. The teacher should inform the children that there will be a discussion about when the pigs were happy or sad. The teacher then reads the story.

   The teacher uses hand puppets to identify the following skills.

   **NOTE:** The ditto for the hand puppet can be found on page 109. To make the puppet, simply have the children color the happy and sad faces, cut out the faces, and glue the circles back to back with a popsicle stick in the middle.

3. ***Identify the Skill Components:*** (list on board)

   1. Tell how you feel—happy or sad.
   2. Say why you feel that way (happy or sad).
   3. Talk about what made you happy or sad.
   4. Say what you can do to change from being sad to being happy.
   5. Share your feelings with a friend, family member, or another adult.

4. ***Model the Skill:*** The teacher models the skill by having a child ask him or her how he or she is feeling. The teacher responds, using the Skill Components to explain the answers. (e.g.: **"Today I feel _____. I feel _____ because _____. I would like to talk about the way I feel. I could change the way I feel by _____. I'm glad I shared my feelings with you."**)

5. ***Behavioral Rehearsal:***

   A. *Selection:* The teacher gives each child a Happy/Sad hand puppet.

B. *Role Play:* The teacher will read different parts in the story of *The Three Little Pigs* and the children will indicate with their hand puppets whether the pigs are happy or sad. The teacher will call on the children to explain why the pig is happy or sad.

C. *Completion:* Reinforce appropriate responses. If incorrect, re-enact or explain.

D. *Reinforcers:* Verbal praise for each child's response.

E. *Discussion:* The teacher will ask the children: **"Who likes to be happy?" "Who likes to be sad?" "When you are sad, what can you do to make yourself happy?"**

6. *Practice:* The teacher selects two children. One child will show a picture card while the other child uses the happy/sad puppet to indicate if the picture makes the child feel happy or sad. A puppet and picture cards could be placed in a learning center. Children and teacher will sing the song on the following page together.

7. *Independent Use:* Give the children a ditto of the happy/sad face to take home. Have the child ask family members how their day was. The family member can use the ditto to relay his or her feelings. Encourage the child to ask "Why?"

8. *Continuation:* Remind the children that being nice to others will help them and others feel good about themselves.

*Suggested Reading*

Aliki. *The Two of Them.* New York: Greenwillow, 1979.

Grifalconi, Ann. *Kinda Blue.* New York: Little Brown, 1993.

Williams, Vera. *A Chair for My Mother.* New York: Greenwillow, 1982.

## "If You're Happy and You Know It"

**Verse One**

If you're happy and you know it, clap your hands (clap, clap)
If you're happy and you know it, clap your hands (clap, clap)
If you're happy and you know it
And you really want to show it,
If you're happy and you know it, clap your hands (clap, clap)

**Verse Two**

If you're happy and you know it, blink your eyes (blink, blink)
If you're happy and you know it, blink your eyes (blink, blink)
If you're happy and you know it
And you really want to show it,
If you're happy and you know it, blink your eyes (blink, blink)

**Other Verses**

**Substitute actions can be:**    touch your ears
give a smile
stand right up
stomp one foot
touch your knee

Name _____

Date _____

HAPPY FACE/SAD FACE STICK PUPPETS

Name _____

Date _____

## SHOW ME HOW YOU FEEL

Color the happy faces a sunny yellow. Color the sad faces blue. Point to each face, one at a time, and name something that makes you *feel* just the way the face looks.

## SOCIAL SKILL
### *Expressing Feelings Openly*

***Behavioral Objective:*** The children will learn to express their feelings openly. The children will learn to respect others' feelings.

***Directed Lesson:***

1. ***Establish the Need:*** The teacher will help children express how they feel. The teacher will ask the child how they felt before coming to school. Each child should be given an opportunity to respond. The teacher will ask the children if they have ever felt lonely or hurt. Give the children an opportunity to share their stories.

2. ***Introduction:*** The teacher will draw three faces on the board. The first face should depict happiness. The second face should depict sadness. The third face should be nondescript.

   The teacher will explain: **"Sometimes we know how others are feeling by the expression on their face. However, sometimes a face does not reveal how a person feels. The person may say 'I don't care.' But, that person may be sad, lonely, or hurt inside. For example, how would you feel if:**

   **1. Your friend broke a leg.**

   **2. You won first place in a race.**

   **3. Your mother got a new car.**

   **4. You were alone in the house.**

   **5. You found ten dollars.**

   **6. No one came to your birthday party."**

   The teacher will use hand puppets to identify the following skills.

3. ***Identify the Skill Components:*** (list on board)

   1. Talk about your feelings.

   2. Ask someone else how they feel.

   3. Say good and kind things to others or do them for others.

   4. Remember to say "I'm sorry" if you say or do something that is unkind.

4.  ***Model the Skill:*** The teacher will use hand puppets or stick figures to demonstrate feelings of happiness and sadness. The children can be encouraged to relate stories depicting sad, happy, or lonely incidents.

5.  ***Behavioral Rehearsal:***

    A. *Selection:* The teacher will select individuals or small groups of children to act out reactions and feelings related to the story starters given in the Introduction.

    B. *Role Play:* The teacher assigns each child a role to act out appropriate feelings in response to one of the examples given in the Introduction.

    C. *Completion:* The teacher asks children to offer suggestions about how to help make a person feel happy instead of lonely or sad.

    D. *Reinforcers:* Verbally reinforce children who did the role play. Praise the children who gave input. Hugs, smiles and non-verbal praise are all appropriate.

    E. *Discussion:* The teacher asks: **"How does it feel if someone hurts your feelings? How does it feel if someone is nice and kind to you? Would you rather have someone hurt your feelings or be nice to you? Why?"**

6.  ***Practice:*** During the daily activities, the children will work on being nice to each other. The teacher recognizes their efforts in a positive manner. The children will put a happy face on the accompanying drawing, "Put On a Happy Face."

7.  ***Independent Use:*** The teacher should let the parents know the skill the class is working on and ask the parents to reinforce good behavior and correct inappropriate behavior in the home setting.

8.  ***Continuation:*** Pick out different children on a weekly basis for being nice to other children. Give them a sticker or a special reward. Have a large yellow smiling face chart, and when directed, children can print their name or first initial right on the face.

*Suggested Reading* (Being friendly)

Barrack, Debra and Sal. *The Adventures of Taxi Dog.* New York: Dial Books for Young Readers, 1990.

Name _____

Date _____

## SOCIAL SKILL
### Recognizing Happy and Sad Feelings

**Behavioral Objective:** The children will demonstrate recognition of happy and sad feelings by showing the appropriate side of a happy/sad face sign when asked to respond to a question about a situation.

**Directed Lesson:**

1. **Establish the Need:** The teacher establishes the need by commenting that it is very important to understand our feelings and know when we are happy or sad and to know when others are happy or sad.

2. **Introduction:** The teacher introduces the story "The Three Little Kittens," asks the class to listen carefully and look at the pictures so they will know when the kittens are happy or sad. After reading the story the teacher asks the children to point out when the kittens are happy or sad and asks for explanation from children of why. She calls attention to the kittens' facial expressions as a means of determining their feelings.

3. **Identify the Skill Components:** (list on board)

   The teacher uses a picture of a kitten glued to a tongue depressor as a hand puppet to identify the following skills for the children:

   1. Sit quietly.
   2. Listen to teacher.
   3. Raise hand to be called on.
   4. Wait to be called on.
   5. Using the sign, show how you would feel.

4. **Model the Skill:** The teacher cuts out one set of happy and sad cat faces on page 116 and glues them to a tongue depressor, one face to each side. The teacher then models the skill for the children by looking at the picture of the kittens, displaying the correct side of the sign, and explaining how we can tell that the kitten is happy or sad and why.

5. **Behavioral Rehearsal:**

   A. *Selection:* The teacher selects a child to hold the happy/sad sign.

    B. *Role Play:* The teacher names a situation which causes sadness or happiness. The child is to display the appropriate side of the sign, then pass it to the next child. Praise is given when the correct side of the picture is shown and assistance given when it is not, followed by reinforcement for correcting the response.

    C. *Completion:* After each role play, reinforce correct behavior, identify inappropriate behaviors, and reenact role play with corrections. If there are no corrections, role play is complete.

    D. *Reinforcers:* During the role play, the teacher will give reinforcement to those who are able to identify the feelings correctly and give verbal explanation. Verbal praise, tangible rewards, group praise, non-verbal praise (i.e., smile, pat, hug) are appropriate.

    E. *Discussion:* How do you know if someone is happy or sad? What does it look like on a person's face? Have a large mirror available so that children can see their happy or unhappy face.

6. **Practice:** The teacher will distribute the worksheet with a happy and sad face. Ask each child to choose one and then tell teacher a story about what made the person happy or sad. The teacher will copy the story on the picture (this only needs to be a sentence or two), and display the picture. They may color the picture.

7. **Independent Use:** Ask parents to tell happy and sad stories and have children retell some of these stories to the class.

8. **Continuation:** The teacher will remind children of the importance of knowing when we are happy or sad, and when others are happy or sad, when related situations arise.

*Suggested Reading (Poetry)*

Pomerantz, Charlotte. *Flap Your Wings and Try.* New York: Wm. Morrow, (Greenwillow), 1989.

Prelutsky, Jack, ed. *For Laughing Out Loud: Poems to Tickle Your Funny Bone.* New York: Knopf, 1991.

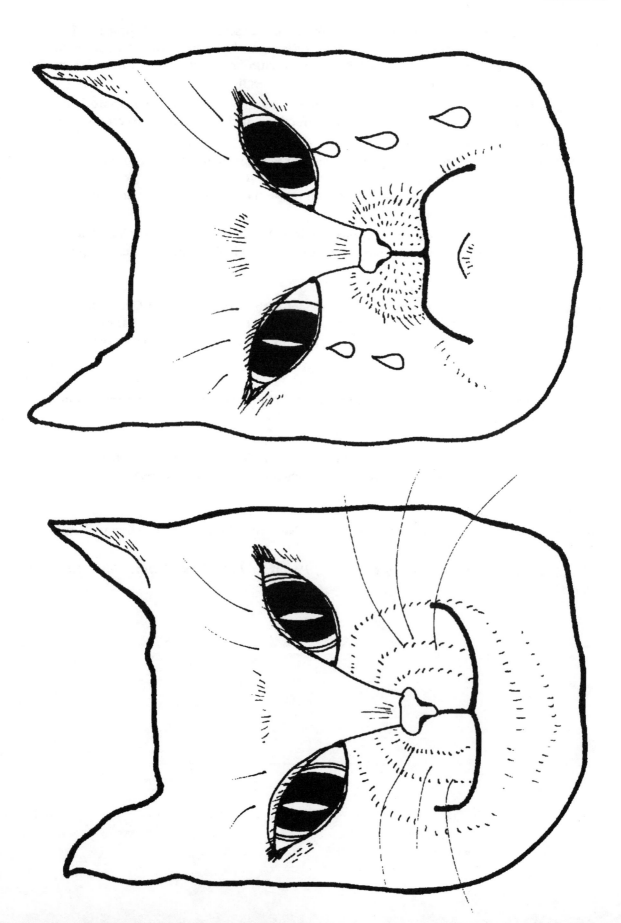

Date _____

Name _____

# SOCIAL SKILL

## *Showing Empathy for the Feelings of Others*

***Behavioral Objective:*** The children will be able to show recognition and empathy for the feelings of other children when they are lonely or hurt.

***Directed Lesson:***

1.  ***Establish the Need:*** The teacher comments that it is important to recognize when we have been hurt by others and when we do something to hurt another person's feelings. If we cannot recognize our feelings and know when we are hurt or lonely and also recognize the feelings of others, we will not know how to prevent ourselves from hurting other people and making them sad, or how to prevent them from hurting our feelings and causing us to be sad or lonely.

2.  ***Introduction:*** The teacher tells the story of three children, Mary, Susan and Bobbie, who played together every day. One day, however, two of the children, Mary and Bobbie, went to the playground and left Susan, who could not go. Susan felt lonely and her feelings were very hurt. The next day Susan brought out her new toy and asked Mary to come into the house to play. This time they left Bobbie outside, sad and lonely because she was not invited to come in to play. After telling the story, *have a discussion* about how Susan and Bobbie felt when they were left alone and what the children could have done to prevent one or the other from being hurt and lonely.

3.  ***Identify the Skill Components:*** (list on board)

    1. Understand the feelings of others.
    2. Treat others the way you want to be treated.
    3. Other people's feelings are hurt as easily as yours.
    4. Do not purposely hurt the feelings of others.
    5. Find ways to make others happy.
    6. Empathize with the feelings of others.

4.  ***Model the Skill:*** The teacher will model the skill by using the skill components and the story in the Introduction to demonstrate to the children how unkind Mary and Bobbie were to Susan by leaving her alone at home. Point out how Bobbie was hurt when Susan invited Mary only, to play with her new toy. The teacher will also indicate that Susan might purposely have

not invited Bobbie because she had been left alone by Bobbie previously. The teacher will encourage and indicate alternatives to prevent hurting others.

5.  **Behavioral Rehearsal:**

    A. *Selection:* The teacher will select a group of children to point out alternatives to children's behavior in the introductory story that will not hurt any children, while the rest of the children will listen and discuss the alternative stories.

    B. *Role Play:* The children are asked to act out the story in the introduction and find ways to make all three friends happy. This could be repeated with another group of children until all children have had a chance to be actors. The teacher should provide other stories to reinforce the need to understand the feelings of others in order not to hurt anyone.

    C. *Completion:* Role play is complete when the children have shown appropriate understanding and the role play needs no corrections.

    D. *Reinforcers:* The teacher praises the "actors" and points out how important it is to understand the feelings of others and how to prevent others from getting hurt.

    E. *Discussion:* The teacher will discuss, again, the skill components and encourage the understanding that alternatives which prevent either child from being hurt are better than trying to pay others back by finding a way of revenge.

6.  **Practice:** The teacher should express the expectation that during their daily activities the children will work hard to be kind and considerate to their classmates. They should remember that they do not like to have their own feelings hurt and therefore, should not hurt others' feelings. They should be encouraged, to some degree, to tell the teacher when they see the proper behavior displayed and to correct their classmates when they see behaviors which will cause someone's feelings to be hurt. The children will be asked to color the worksheet for this lesson on the following page.

7.  **Independent Use:** The children will use the skills they have learned to be considerate and kind to their parents and others they meet, in order not to hurt their feelings.

8.  **Continuation:** Teacher will remind children of the importance of recognizing and showing sympathy for the feelings of others when they have been hurt, as related situations arise.

*Suggested Reading* (Feelings)

Bunting, Eve. *Valentine Bears*. Boston: Houghton Mifflin, 1985.

Duvoisin, Roger. *Our Veronica Goes to Petunia's Farm*. New York: Knopf.

Name _____ Date _____

PLAY FAIR, AND TREAT OTHERS AS
YOU WOULD LIKE TO BE TREATED.

# ACCEPTING DIFFERENCES

## SOCIAL SKILL

*Understanding Differences and Similarities*

**Behavioral Objective:** The children will learn to understand that uniqueness is common to all people. The children will learn that we are all alike and yet different in many ways.

**Directed Lesson:**

1. **Establish the Need:** The teacher establishes the importance of recognizing and accepting differences and similarities of the children. There is a word to describe differences. That word is "special."

2. **Introduction:** The teacher discusses with the class the differences that they can see about each other (e.g.: size, hair color, eye color, etc.) as well as things that are the same.

   The teacher then reads the following poem, inserting names of children in the class. The children in the class listen carefully while the poem is read.

   > **"Bobby is short and Billy is tall.**
   > **Sherry wears glasses, and Amy none at all.**
   > **But we are all children who like to have fun.**
   > **We all like to skip and jump and run.**
   >
   > **Jaenin's hair is red and Jason's is brown**
   > **Mary's hair stands up and Becky's hangs down.**
   > **We are all children who live in this town.**
   > **We're all different, yet we're all the same,**
   > **So let's all be friends and just say our name!"**

   (Go around the circle and have each child say his/her name as the groups claps in rhythm.)

   The teacher uses hand puppets to identify the following skills.

3. **Identify the Skill Components:** (list on board)
   1. Accept different physical characteristics.
   2. Learn that physical differences do not affect friendships.
   3. Learn that in spite of physical differences, we are more alike than different.
   4. Learn that each child is special and can be proud of being unique.

4. **Model the Skill:** The teacher will reread the poem with the puppets to emphasize to the children the differences and similarities in people.

121

**5.   *Behavioral Rehearsal:***

    A. *Selection:* Choose a group of about four children with different characteristics and adapt the poem in the Introduction to their characteristics. At the end of the poem, ask each child: **"But are you a special person?" "Do you like to play?" "Do you like to have fun?"**

    B. *Role Play:* Ask each child in the selected group to name a similarity or a difference between him or herself and another member in the selected group.

    C. *Completion:* After the role play, the teacher may point out similarities and differences which were not mentioned.

    D. *Reinforcers:* The teacher praises "actors" and points out a special quality of each child.

    E. *Discussion:* The teacher will ask the children who did not role play for additional observations on similarities and differences.

**6.   *Practice:*** Observe pictures of different groups of animals, such as horses, dogs, cats, cows, birds, pigs, etc. Point out differences in color, size and other physical characteristics. Also, emphasize similar needs such as the need for food, the need for sleep, the need for safety. The teacher asks the children to color the following worksheet and point out the differences and similarities among the five faces.

**7.   *Independent Use:*** The teacher re-emphasizes that similarities and differences can be identified and appreciated throughout the year at home with family, friends and peers.

**8.   *Continuation:*** Throughout the school year the teacher reminds and helps the children to accept differences in each other.

*Suggested Reading*

Duvoisin, Roger. *Petunia.* New York: Knopf Books for Young Readers, 1962.

Wells, Rosemary. *Shy Charles.* New York: Dial Books for Young Readers, 1988.

Wildsmith, Brian. *The Little Wood Duck.* New York: Franklin Watts, 1972.

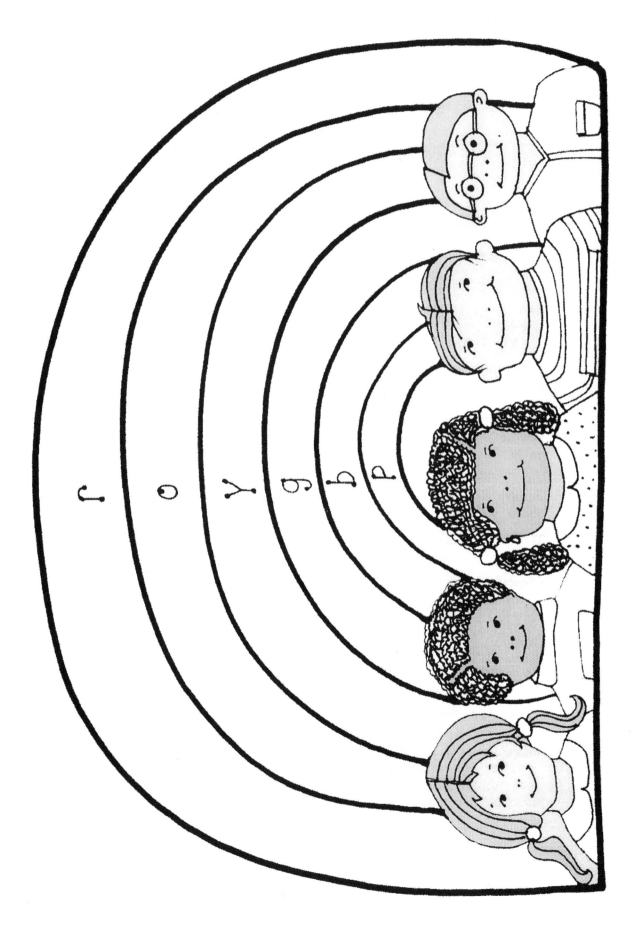

# SOCIAL SKILL

*Recognizing and Accepting Cultural Differences*

**Behavioral Objective:** The children will respect all people of the world by recognizing and accepting the cultural differences that exist.

**Directed Lesson:**

1. **Establish the Need:** Children need to know that the world is composed of people who have different cultural habits. Cultural differences need to be recognized, appreciated and respected.

2. **Introduction:** Use a variety of pictures that depict different cultural environments (i.e., deserts, mountains, islands, villages, crowded cities, etc.) and the people who live in these environments. The teacher will introduce the concept that people all over the world live, dress, travel, eat, work and play in different ways. Even though these people and their ways of life are different, we need to respect them and their differences.

   The teacher will ask the children: **"What does it mean to respect someone who, for example, wears different styles of clothing?"** Apply the children's answers to the above concept.

   The teacher will use hand puppets to identify the following skills.

3. **Identify the Skill Components:** (list on board)
   1. Respect people who look different.
   2. Respect people who live in different ways.
   3. Respect people who eat and like different foods.
   4. Respect people who are dressed differently.
   5. Respect people who speak a different language.
   6. Help children who have difficulties because they do things differently than you.

4. **Model the Skill:** The teacher points out that respect can be shown for all types of people by willingly accepting people with their differences. To demonstrate this, the teacher models the skill by using one of the cultural pictures from the Introduction and making complimentary remarks and observations about the different aspects of the pictured culture.

**5.  *Behavioral Rehearsal:***

>    A. *Selection:* The teacher will select two children to discuss a given picture. When the pair is finished discussing, another pair can be selected for the next picture. Selection of children may continue as long as appropriate.
>
>    B. *Role Play:* Using the picture, the children will describe what they see and what they like in the picture. They will tell what the people in the pictures are doing and how the children feel about them by comparing the people in the picture with themselves.
>
>    C. *Completion:* Role play is complete when children have exhausted their observations and reactions to the picture.
>
>    D. *Reinforcers:* Verbal praise is given to the pairs of children who discussed the pictures in the role play.
>
>    E. *Discussion:* Ask the listening group for any additional information about the picture. Also ask them how they feel when comparing themselves with the people in the picture. (This discussion should follow each picture discussed by a pair of students.)

**6.  *Practice:*** During the school year, bring in food, songs and games of different cultures.

**7.  *Independent Use:*** Ask children to talk to their parents about different cultures, especially about their families' cultural background.

**8.  *Continuation:*** Reinforce the concept of acceptance and respect for those who are different throughout the school year with books, songs, games, etc.

*Suggested Reading*

Burningham, John. *Hey! Get Off Our Train.* New York: Crown Books for Young Readers, 1990.

Leventhal, Debra. *What Is Your Language?* New York: Dutton, 1993.

Polacco, Patricia. *Chicken Sunday.* New York: Putnam Publishing Group, 1992.

## SOCIAL SKILL
### *Accepting the Uniqueness of Each Person*

**Behavioral Objective:** The children will learn each person is unique. They will further learn to understand that we are also alike in many ways. However, we must accept each other for our individual differences.

**Directed Lesson:**

1.  **Establish the Need:** The teacher establishes the importance of recognizing differences with the following comments, **"We are all different; we have different hair color, eye color, height, weight, parents, homes, brothers, sisters, etc. There is a special word to describe differences: the word is *Unique*."**

2.  **Introduction:** Teacher discusses with the class the uniqueness of each of them; ie., family size, position in family, sex, ages, occupations of parents, goals of students, living quarters, etc.

    After the discussion, the teacher will ask the children to recognize how each of them is different in relation to each other. Does this make them better or worse? No, it makes each one unique.

3.  **Identify the Skill Components:** (List on board or sentence strips)

    1. Accept that everyone is different and therefore unique.
    2. Make friends with someone who is different.
    3. Find something you like about a friend who is different.

4.  **Model the Skill:** Teacher models skill by recognizing differences in children and showing appreciation of differences; i.e., if all looked alike and had the same name, how could they be different?

5.  **Behavioral Rehearsal:**

    A. *Selection:* Teacher selects two children to participate in the role play.
    B. *Role Play:* Using a story or picture (worksheet), the teacher asks the children to describe the differences between the characters in the story or picture (worksheet). Then the children in the class describe the differences between the children who are doing the role play.

      C. *Completion:* After each role play, reinforce correct behavior, identify inappropriate behavior and re-enact role play with corrections. If there are no corrections, role play is complete.

      D. *Reinforcers:* During the role play, the teacher will give reinforcement to those who are able to identify the similarities and differences between the children and cite the benefits of each.

      E. *Discussion:* Why is it important to be different and to accept the differences in others?

6. **Practice:** Children will draw a picture of themselves and their best friend on copies of the following worksheet. They will share with the class likenesses and differences.

7. **Independent Use:** Children will take home the pictures they drew and explain to an adult at home the Social Skill learned at school.

8. **Continuation:** Teacher should continue pointing out the need for this skill as related situations arise.

Name _____ Date _____

## MY FRIEND IS LIKE ME IN SOME WAYS

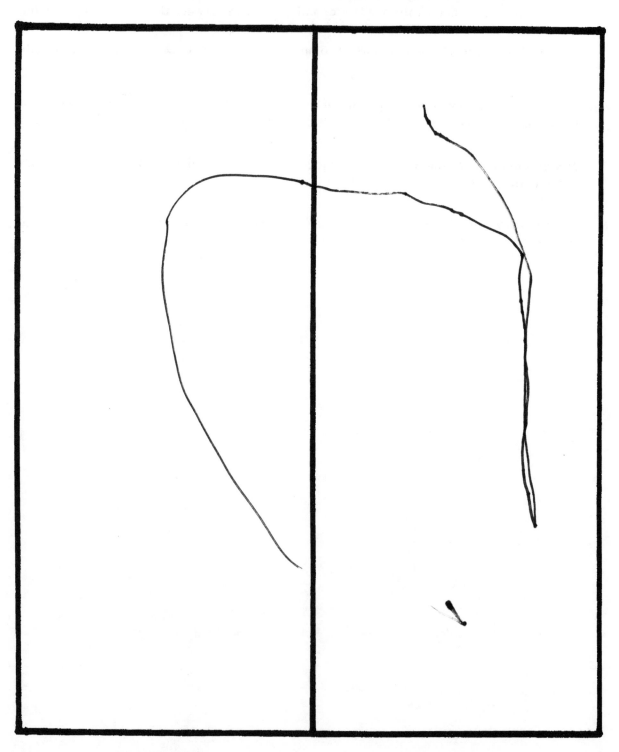

THIS IS ME.                    THIS IS MY FRIEND.

## SOCIAL SKILL
### *Learning to Cooperate*

**Behavioral Objective:** The children will learn to cooperate by being helpful to one another, being good sports, and being kind.

### *Directed Lesson:*

1.  ***Establish the Need:*** The teacher will establish the need to learn to cooperate by stating: **"Girls and boys, when we play a game, it is important that we cooperate so no one gets hurt or feels sad and left out. We can cooperate by being a good sport. A good sport is kind and helpful."**

2.  ***Introduction:*** The teacher will say:

    **"Boys and girls, let's try a game of Follow the Leader. We will have one line and a leader. I will be the leader and I have a rope. We will use the rope to keep us in line. The leader will need your cooperation. When I call your name, please come over carefully and hold the rope. When everyone is holding the rope, I will need you to look at me. ('One, Two, Three, Look at me!') Let me show you how we will play the game. First, I will hold the rope with my left hand, then I will look straight ahead and begin to walk slowly. If you can do that, then we are ready for our walk around the school. Let's go!"**

    The teacher uses hand puppets to identify the following skills.

3.  ***Identify the Skill Components:*** (list on board)

    1. Listen to directions.
    2. Wait for your turn.
    3. Join the group activity proudly.
    4. Be kind and helpful to others in the group.
    5. Be happy.

4.  ***Model the Skill:*** The teacher selects six children to model the skill. Review Skill Components during this time.

**5.   *Behavioral Rehearsal:***

> A. *Selection:* The teacher selects eight children to do the role play.

> B. *Role Play:* The eight children will practice the walking game with the rope.

> C. *Completion:* After each role play, reinforce correct behavior and identify inappropriate behavior. Re-enact role play with corrections. Role play is then complete.

> D. *Reinforcers:* The teacher shakes each child's hand and says: **"Congratulations! You are a good sport. You know how to cooperate!"**

> E. *Discussion:* **"It was nice to see that everyone remembered to cooperate. Everyone walked slowly and no one let go of the rope. What 'good sports' you are! How does it feel to cooperate?"**

**6.   *Practice:*** The children can practice this skill when they play ball, share the scissors, etc.

**7.   *Independent Use:*** The children can use this skill during clean up time at school. At home they can cooperate by helping with the family chores.

**8.   *Continuation:*** The teacher will use verbal praise when children practice this skill.

*Suggested Reading*

Lionni, Leo. *Swimmy.* New York: Knopf Books for Young Readers, 1987.

Williams, Jay. *The Reward Worth Having.* New York: Macmillan, 1977.

## SOCIAL SKILL
### *Learning to Take Turns*

***Behavioral Objective:*** The children will learn to take turns during school activities. The children will learn that they cannot always be first.

***Directed Lesson:***

1. ***Establish the Need:*** The teacher will establish the need for learning to take turns by stating: **"Boys and girls, it is important to learn to take turns because each one of us likes to be first. We all like to play with the same toys and we all like to be served our food first. Therefore, we must take turns so each of us gets a chance to be first."**

2. ***Introduction:*** **"Boys and girls, today we are going to play a game of bean bag toss. We will have two groups. Everyone will get a turn, but you may not be first right away. I'll show you how we will play the game. First, I stand on the tape. I will toss the bean bag three times into the bucket. I will stay on the tape. Watch me. Now, it is your turn."** (Select one child.)

   The teacher uses hand puppets to identify the following skills.

3. ***Identify the Skill Components:*** (list on board)

      1. Stand or sit quietly.
      2. Listen to the teacher.
      3. Remain at assigned place.
      4. Wait patiently for your turn.

4. ***Model the Skill:*** The teacher will select two children to model the skill. Review Skill Components at this time.

5. ***Behavioral Rehearsal:***
      A. *Selection:* The teacher selects six children to do the role play.
      B. *Role Play:* The six children will practice the game in sequence. They will stand in line and wait until they are the first to play the game.
      C. *Completion:* After each role play, reinforce correct behavior. If needed, re-enact role play with corrections. Role play is then complete.

D. *Reinforcers:* The teacher shakes each child's hand and says: **"Thank you for taking turns."**

E. *Discussion:* **"It was nice that everyone was able to have a turn. You stood straight in line. No one pushed. How does it feel to be first and last?"**

6.   *Practice:* The children can practice this skill by taking turns setting the table, being first on a walk, etc.

7.   *Independent Use:* The children can take turns riding their tricycles with their brothers or sisters or take turns with toys at school.

8.   *Continuation:* The teacher will use verbal praise when children practice this skill.

*Suggested Reading*

Cox, David. *Bossyboots.* New York: Crown, 1987.

Ketteman, Helen. *Not Yet, Yvette.* New York: A. Whitman, 1992.

# ATTENDING TO TASK

## SOCIAL SKILL
### *Ignoring Distractions*

*Behavioral Objective:* The children will demonstrate the ability to continue in an activity while other activities are going on around them.

*Directed Lesson:*

1.  *Establish the Need:* The teacher introduces the skill: **"We need to learn to work while people around us are doing other things. If we always stop our work to watch another person, we will not be able to finish and we will not learn how to do things."** Teacher involves children in a discussion of this skill and its importance. For example, if you are working at the language table and someone comes over to ask the teacher a question, are you supposed to stop and talk to that person? etc.

2.  *Introduction:* Teacher asks children to close their eyes and listen to the sounds around them. Teacher will list the sounds on the board. Ask children what sounds bother them while they're working. Put an "X" in front of those sounds.

3.  *Identify the Skill Components:* (list on board)

    The teacher identifies the skill components for the children.

    > 1. You choose or are called on to do an activity.
    > 2. You begin that activity.
    > 3. You keep working even if there are sounds all around you.

4.  *Model the Skill:* The teacher models the skill by taking an activity such as a puzzle, and asking a child to get another activity and begin to work nearby. The teacher does not stop putting the puzzle together until it is completed.

5.  *Behavioral Rehearsal:*

    A. *Selection:* The teacher selects a few children to perform and several to be the observers.

    B. *Role Play:* One child chooses an activity and brings it before the group. While he/she is doing this the teacher instructs another child to get an activity and sit nearby and two others to get books, sit nearby and read together. When and if the first child completes the activity without being distracted, the role play is completed.

    C. *Completion:* After each role play, reinforce correct behavior, identify inappropriate behaviors, and reenact role play with corrections. If there are no corrections, role play is complete.

    D. *Reinforcers:* The teacher gives praise for the responses which demonstrate comprehension and the importance of working without being distracted.

    E. *Discussion:* The teacher asks questions which help the children to evaluate the role play. Did the first child look up from her work? Did he/she stop working when the others came near?

6.   **Practice:** Make copies of coloring sheets #1 through #5 on the following pages. Use coloring sheet #1 as practice for learning to work while ignoring distractions.

    The worksheets are numbered according to difficulty. Use the remaining worksheets over a period of several days with the whole class or small groups. Sheet #1 is to occupy the children for about one minute, Sheet #2 for two, etc. until the children demonstrate the ability to work for at least five minutes without paying attention to distractions. *Directions:* The children will be instructed to color the sheets while the teacher walks around the room and talks to herself or sings. (The children are not to look up at the teacher or stop working!)

7.   **Independent Use:** Ask children to draw a picture at home while the T.V. is on. Ask them to continue working and to ignore the T.V. Bring the picture to school and discuss.

8.   **Continuation:** The teacher continues to remind children to pay attention to their own work and ignore distractions as related situations arise.

*Suggested Reading*

Brown, Marcia. *How, Hippo!* New York: Scribner, 1969.

dePaola, Tomie. *Strega Nona.* Englewood Cliffs, NJ: Prentice Hall, 1975.

Name _____ Date _____

Name _____ Date _____

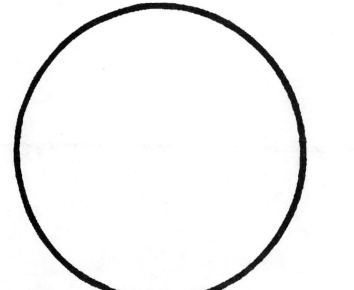

Name _____ Date _____

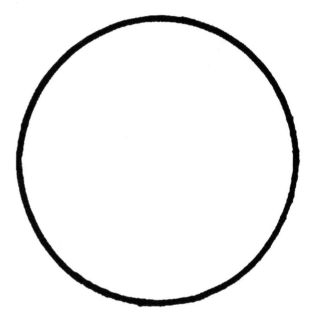

Name _____ Date _____

Name _____

Date _____

## SOCIAL SKILL
### *Solving Problems Peaceably*

**Behavioral Objective:** The children will learn to solve their problems by using appropriate language and peaceful means. The children will make-up by shaking hands.

**Directed Lesson:**

1. **Establish the Need:** The teacher will ask the children if they have ever had a problem with a friend or a sister or brother. Allow the children to give examples. Ask the children how they solved their problem. The teacher will point out that learning to deal with conflicts is needed to avoid more serious problems.

2. **Introduction:** Using two puppets, the teacher will demonstrate a conflict involving sharing. After the demonstration, the teacher will ask the children, **"What could the puppets have done to avoid having this problem happen?"**

   The teacher will use hand puppets to identify the following skills.

3. **Identify the Skill Components:** (list on board)

   1. Think about the problem and calm down.
   2. Say what the problem is.
   3. Discuss how to solve the problem.
   4. Solve the problem in a peaceful way.
   5. Shake hands and be friends.

4. **Model the Skill:** The teacher models the skill by using the two puppets. The teacher will demonstrate how to solve a problem by using the Skill Components.

5. **Behavioral Rehearsal:**

   A. *Selection:* The teacher selects pairs of children. The teacher gives one child of each pair a doll or puppet and suggests a problem to be solved without conflict.
   B. *Role Play:* Each pair of children will find a way to solve the problem by using the Skill Components. After solving the problem in a peaceful manner, they will shake hands. Have each pair of children briefly tell the class how they solved the problem.

      C. *Completion:* Discuss with the children whether or not the chosen way of solving the conflict was appropriate. Reinforce correct behavior and identify inappropriate behavior. Re-enact role play if necessary.

      D. *Reinforcers:* Verbal praise, special compliments, and hugs will be given to the "actors."

      E. *Discussion:* The teacher will ask the children, **"Why is it important to solve your problems in a peaceful way?"**

6. ***Practice:*** The teacher will remind children to solve problems peacefully during daily activities.

7. ***Independent Use:*** Have the children practice the skill at home with their family, siblings and friends as well as at school.

8. ***Continuation:*** The teacher will tell the children that using this skill can help make them feel good about themselves because they will solve many problems in a peaceful way.

*Suggested Reading*

Demuth, Patricia Brennan. *The Ornery Morning*. New York: Dutton, 1991.

Henkes, Kevin. *Julius, the Baby of the World*. New York: Wm. Morrow (Greenwillow), 1990.

## SOCIAL SKILL

### *How to Communicate to Make Friends*

**Behavioral Objective:** The children will learn to communicate and make friends through words, compliments, gestures, hugs, pictures, and songs.

**Directed Lesson:**

1. **Establish the Need:** The teacher will say, **"Boys and girls, today we are going to talk about friends. Why do we need friends?"** Allow the children time to answer. After the children have responded, the teacher will say, **"That's right. We need friends because (list some reasons children gave). We also need friends so we have someone to talk to and share our feelings with. There's a word we can use which means 'talking, sharing feelings, and telling people things about what we do.' This word is 'Communicate.' Talking is just one way we communicate. Can anyone think of any others?"** (sign language, pictures, a hug, a smile, doing something nice for someone.)

2. **Introduction:** (Continuation of discussion) The teacher says, **"Very good! Those are different ways we can <u>communicate</u> with our friends. But, before we can communicate with our friends, we have to make friends. How do you make a friend?"** Allow the children time to answer. The teacher says, **"Those are all very good answers. Another way we can make friends is by saying something nice to someone. For example, I can say 'I like your shirt.' Or 'You are pretty.' We call nice words like these 'Compliments.'"**

3. **Identify the Skill Components:** (list on board)

    1. Decide whom you want as a friend.
    2. Try to start a conversation, perhaps by giving a compliment.
    3. Pick an activity to share with the child you want to have as a friend.
    4. Tell each other about your feelings. (What makes you happy? sad? frightened? etc.).

4. **Model the Skill:** The teacher will model the skill by cutting out five or six pictures (from magazines) of people communicating through gestures, actions or words. The teacher will show each picture to the children and ask the children:

    **"What might the people in the picture be communicating about by their words or gestures? Are they complimenting each other? Are the people in the picture making friends with each other? Why? Or why not?"** Allow children time to respond and discuss their answers.

**5.**   ***Behavioral Rehearsal:***

      A. *Selection:* The teacher will divide the children into pairs to work together on the role play activity. During their role play activity, the pairs of children will communicate with each other using the Skill Components.

      B. *Role Play:* In pairs, the children will find and cut out pictures which show the different ways to make friends and the different ways friends communicate.

      C. *Completion:* The children will place the pictures in a pile, and the teacher will display them on the bulletin board.

      D. *Reinforcers:* The teacher will give verbal praise and compliments to the children for communicating while they work and for completing the task.

      E. *Discussion:* Each pair of children will go to the bulletin board and point to their pictures. The pair of children will discuss the communication involved. (The teacher may want to prompt the children, using the questions found in Model the Skill.) When the pair is finished discussing their pictures, the class will applaud and give compliments to the presenters.

**6.**   ***Practice***: The teacher will leave the magazines for the children to look through. The children may cut out more communication pictures for the teacher to place on the bulletin board in a collage. The children will be asked to color a copy of the following worksheet entitled "My Friends Are Special" Song.

**7.**   ***Independent Use:*** The teacher will teach the children to sing the following song and encourage the children to teach the song to their family members. The song is sung to the tune of "Are You Sleeping?" The children will be permitted to take the coloring worksheet home after they have colored it.

**8.**   ***Continuation:*** The teacher will say, **"If you learn to communicate, you will always have friends."** The teacher should continue to point out the need for this skill as related situations arise.

*Suggested Reading* (Friendship)

    Flack, Marjorie. *Angus and the Cat*. New York: Doubleday, 1989.

    Wildsmith, Brian. *Python's Party*. New York: Oxford University Press, 1987.

    Lionni, Leo. *Swimmy*. New York: Knopf Books for Young Readers, 1987.

**"FRIENDS ARE SPECIAL"**
**(Tune: "Are You Sleeping?")**

Friends are special.
Friends are special.
Yes we are.
Yes we are.
** We take turns when talking,
** We hold hands when walking,
We need friends.
We need friends.

**     NOTE: These two lines may be substituted by the following:

A.     We like to do sharing,
      We like to do caring,

B.     We like to give hugs,
      Filled with lots of love,

C.     We can say some nice things,
      Very, very nice things,

D.     We can sing together,
      Sing in any weather,

Name _____

Date _____

# MY "FRIENDS ARE SPECIAL" SONG

Friends are special
Friends are special
Yes we are.
Yes we are.

We take turns when talking,
We hold hands when walking,
We need friends
We need friends.

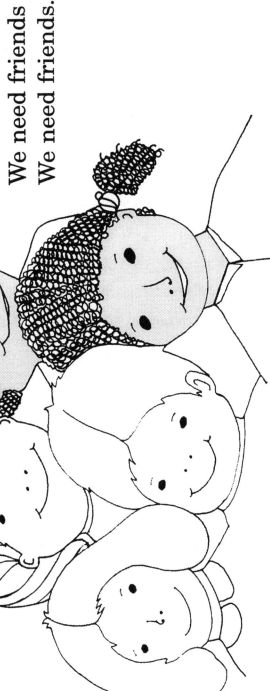

## SOCIAL SKILL

*Saying "NO!" to Negative Peer Pressure*

***Behavioral Objective:*** The children will say "NO!" when asked to do something they know is not right or when asked to do something they do not like to do. The will learn when it's O.K. to say no and to be nice when they say no. They will learn the negative and positive aspect of peer pressure and what "peer pressure" means. (Negative peer pressure is not wanting to do something because you know it's wrong, and yet you see others doing it and they want you to join them.)

***Directed Lesson:***

1.  ***Establish the Need:*** The teacher will help the children deal with negative peer pressure by saying "NO!" in a nice way and by stating: **"Boys and girls, there is something I want to talk to you about. It's about friends. We all have friends. We like to play with our friends, but sometimes, friends want us to do something that is not right or something we don't like to do. When this happens, it's O.K. to say 'NO!' Be nice but firm when you say 'NO!'**

    **"Positive Peer Pressure is different. Friends might ask you to participate in an interesting activity or in a game. In this case, you might want to say 'YES!'"**

2.  ***Introduction:*** **"Today boys and girls, we are going to play a game to decide if negative or positive peer pressure is applied. We will use the tape recorder for our game. We will work in small groups, but everyone will get a turn. I am going to ask you some questions and if the answer is no, I want you to say "NO!" into the tape recorder. The questions\* are about your friends. I will start the game. The tape recorder is <u>on</u>. My question is: My friends want me to play in the street, but I'm not sure. I'm worried about the cars. What should I say?"** (The children respond: "NO!") Play this back so that the child can hear it. **"The tape recorder is <u>off</u>. Saying no to playing in the street was the right thing to say. Now, let's give the next person a turn."** The teacher continues to ask questions until all children have had a chance to respond.

    The teacher uses hand puppets to identify the following skills:

3.  ***Identify the Skill Components:*** (list on board)

    1. Decide if you want to participate.

    2. Decide if the peer pressure is good or bad (positive or negative).

    3. If you think the peer pressure is bad, say "NO!"

\*See suggested questions on page 149.

4. If you think the peer pressure is good, say "YES!"

5. Be nice, but firm, when you say "no."

4. **Model the Skill:** The teacher asks for two volunteers to model the skill. Review Skill Components during this time.

5. **Behavioral Rehearsal:**

   A. *Selection:* The teacher selects four children to role play. (The teacher helps with the tape recorder and if necessary, with a question—but the child will ask the question, not the teacher.)

   B. *Role Play:* The four children will practice the game by asking questions dealing with negative (bad) as well as with positive (good) peer pressure.

   C. *Completion:* After each role play, reinforce correct behavior and identify inappropriate behavior. Re-enact role play with corrections if necessary. Role play is then complete.

   D. *Reinforcers:* The teacher tapes a personal message to each child. **"Bruce, I like the way you sat. You were so quiet." "Shivanna, you sounded firm when you said no."**

   E. *Discussion:* **"It's hard to say no to our friends, but we can't let them make us do something that we know is not right. How do you feel about saying "NO!" to a friend?"**

6. **Practice:** The teacher will have a "NO Box" and "NO Cards" in easy reach of the children. Instruct the children to go over and put a "NO Card" in the box whenever they think a friend "pressures" them to do something they don't want or like to do. (The "NO Box" and cards take the place of the tape recorder.)

7. **Independent Use:** The children can use this skill in their daily interactions with their peers in school situations. For home use, the teacher may send a note home with the child. An example of such a note is shown on the following page.

8. **Continuation:** The teacher shakes child's hand when child practices this skill. Since saying no to negative peer pressure is difficult and it takes more practice than saying yes to positive peer pressure.

*Suggested Reading*

Numeroff, Laura Joffe. *If You Give a Mouse a Cookie.* New York: Harper Collins Children's Books, 1985.

*If You Give a Moose a Muffin, Big Book.* New York: Harper Collins Children's Books, 1991.

Dear Family:

Hello!

I'm learning to say "NO!" when I know something is not right and when my friends and peers use negative peer pressure to make me join them in doing things that I was told not to do.

Will you help me?

Love,

William

## Suggested Questions

### Dealing with Negative Peer Pressure

My friend wants me to play with matches. Should I?

My friend says it's O.K. to swear. Is it?

My friend wants to take the money. Should I?

My friend wants to throw stones at a car. Should I?

My friend says, "Hit him!" Should I?

My friend says, "It's O.K. to lie." Should I?

My friend says, "It's O.K. to smoke." Is it?

My friend says, "It's O.K. to yell at someone." Is it?

My friend says, "It's O.K. to break the toy." Is it?

My friend says, "It's O.K. to spit on the floor." Is it?

## SOCIAL SKILL

*Making Independent Choices Despite Peer Pressure*

**Behavioral Objective:** The children can make independent choices despite pressure of peers to follow their choice.

**Directed Lesson:**

1. **Establish the Need:** The teacher comments: **"Boys and girls, everyone must learn to choose and make decisions for themselves. Sometimes others may want you to do what they want, but if that is not what you want to do, it is very important to make you own decision. That is, decide for yourself what you want to do. If we do not learn to do this, then we will always be following someone else. We will never have the chance to do things that we feel are important and that we like to do the best."**

2. **Introduction:** The teacher tells the following story:

   **"Once there were three little girls who were best friends. Everyday they worked and played everywhere together. One day one of the little girls wanted to do something else that the other two little girls did not want to do. The other two girls said that they would no longer be her friend. The little girl cried and was worried because she wanted to be the other girls' friend but she also wanted to do something else that day. When her teacher saw her crying and found out why she was crying, the teacher talked to all of the little girls. He/she told them that it was all right for one of them to do something the others did not want to do, and that they could still remain friends and work together again when they wanted to do the same things. The little girls were glad to know that they could make independent choices and still remain friends."**

   The teacher and class discuss the story.

3. **Identify the Skill Components:** (list on board)

   The teacher uses a hand puppet to identify the skill components for the children.

   1. Think of what you want to do.
   2. Listen to your friends.
   3. Make your own choice.
   4. Tell your friends what you have decided.

4.  ***Model the Skill:*** The teacher models the skill for the children, voicing his/her decision aloud to show an independent choice different from that his/her friends want him/her to do when on vacation.

5.  ***Behavioral Rehearsal:***

    A. *Selection:* The teacher selects three children.

    B. *Role Play:* Two of the children are instructed to try to get the other to do what they want to do. But the third one is instructed to demonstrate the skills involved in making an independent choice.

    C. *Completion:* After each role play, reinforce correct behavior, identify inappropriate behaviors, and reenact role play with corrections. If there are no corrections, role play is complete.

    D. *Reinforcers:* The teacher gives praise for responses that demonstrate understanding, and encourages the children to resist peer pressure.

    E. *Discussion:* Is it hard to make your own choices if friends want you to do things their way?

6.  ***Practice:*** Y-Principle: Teacher makes a large "Y" on the board. All students travel down the same road in school. But eventually they are going to have to stop at a point and make a decision. They can go the "left" way because that's the road a lot of children take, or they can go the "right" way and do what they think is best. Questions: Would you rather follow everyone else or be yourself and go your own way?

    Have the children color the worksheet. Have them make their own choices or a one, two, and three choice.

7.  ***Independent Use:*** The children will have copies of the following coloring sheet showing a picture of three children with caption "I like you, but I am me!" Have them color this sheet, take it home to discuss with family and friends, then bring it back to school and report their decision.

8.  ***Continuation:*** The teacher will stress the importance of making our own choices rather than simply "following the crowd" as related situations arise.

*Suggested Reading*

Hoffman, Mary. *Amazing Grace.* New York: Dial, 1991.

Naylor, Phyllis Reynolds. *King of the Playground.* New York: Atheneum Children's Books, 1991.

Name _____ Date _____

## Make Your Own Choices

Draw a line from the numbers to the food that is your first, second, and third choice. Compare your choices with those of your classmates. Use your crayons to make the food look tasty.

Lesson 50

© 1995 by SPV

# I Like You, but I Am Me.

Sorry, I decided to do something else now, and can't play ball at present with both of you.

Name _____   Date _____

Part I presents 21 social skills-related topics on cards for teacher-led class discussions during Circle Time. Each topic can be introduced once before studying a particular skill, such as listening, and later after the lesson, to assess children's learning.

**NOTE: The topics are printed in the form of discussion cards which can be photocopied and cut out for use at the appropriate time.**

# SOCIAL SKILLS TASK REVIEW

# Part I

Why are social skills important?

**Social skills are important because their frequent use and application determines how well we get along with other people.**

What are they?

| | |
|---|---|
| *respect for others* | *kindness* |
| *listening* | *politeness* |
| *following directions* | *self-control* |
| *sharing* | *cooperation* |
| *consideration* | *patience* |
| *caring* | *problem solving* |
| *accepting change* | *conflict solving peacefully* |

Listening is important because . . .

**Listening is important because if we do not listen when other people speak to us, we will never learn what they are telling us or know how to do something they may be showing us.**

We need to listen carefully at these times:

Fire drill
When teacher gives a listen signal
When teacher gives directions
Any time teacher or family have to say something

Completing assignments is important because . . .

**It is important to finish any job that you choose or are given in order to learn how to do things and how to do them well.**

Discuss the importance of finishing things we start. The format can be, "What would happen if . . . "

- the road was only half finished
- the school bus had a flat tire that wasn't fixed
- the pizza was only half cooked, etc.

Why is it important to pay attention and not let other things distract you?

**It is important to pay attention to what we are doing so that we can finish our work and learn how to do things.**

What are we learning at school?

- how to paint
- how to put things away
- how to sit quietly and listen to a story, etc.
- how to make friends
- how to solve problems (conflicts) peacefully
- how to be helpful to others
- how to use magic courtesy words

---

It is important to follow instructions and directions because . . .

**It is important to follow directions or instructions from your teacher or parents in order to prevent mistakes or accidents and to learn how to do things correctly and safely.**

Why do we *walk* indoors and *run* outdoors?

---

Whose advice do you trust? Why?

**Ex.  I trust my mother's/father's/other relative's advice because she/he loves me and has my best interests at heart.**

What advice do we give to someone who is

- crossing the street
- holding a pet
- being called by a stranger
- being talked to by a stranger, etc.

How do you settle conflicts without violence?

Ex. **We can talk about the problem and try to reach a compromise.**

**We can ask someone else to listen to both sides of the conflict and tell us what they think is fair.**

**One of us can give in to the other or negotiate a different solution.**

How can you avoid getting into a fight?

Ex. **I can avoid getting into a fight by controlling my anger.**

**I can stop and count to ten when I feel myself growing very angry.**

**I can tell my teacher/relative about the problem instead of fighting.**

It takes a lot of practice to learn to handle conflicts constructively. Let's try these things today:

(1) **Think before you speak.**

(2) **Speak in a quiet voice no matter how angry you may feel inside.**

Why is it important to be a good sport and accept consequences in a graceful manner?

Ex. **It shows that you are a good sport.**

**It sets a good example for others.**

**It makes you a better person.**

**It keeps you from fighting and getting hurt.**

**It teaches you to follow the rules.**

How do you react when you fail at something?

Ex. **I feel disappointed and frustrated.**

**I promise myself that I will try again and succeed the next time.**

**I am embarrassed.**

**I will try to learn from failing not to fail again.**

What we think about ourselves is very important. What do you *think* when someone tells you that you did a very good job?

Ex. **I think they are complimenting me on my good work.**

**I think they are encouraging me to keep up the good work.**

**I think I will try harder to do good work.**

I think . . .

How do you *feel* when someone tells you that you did a very good job?

Ex. **I feel proud of myself.**

**I feel good about myself.**

**I feel happy that my work pleases them.**

I feel . . .

How can we show understanding of another's feelings?

Ex. **When someone is hurt we can . . .**

**When someone is crying we can . . .**

**When someone falls down we can . . .**

**When someone spills something we can . . .**

It helps to talk over feelings with other people you trust. If you felt bad about something, who could you talk with?

Ex. **I could talk about it with my mom/dad because she/he would understand how I felt and help me feel less bad.**

Who else can we talk to? At home? At school?

How do you feel when you get a deserved compliment? How can we compliment others? Let's try. We can begin with the words:

"I like the way _____"

"I like it when _____"

---

It is important to ask permission politely if you want to borrow anything. Why? How can we put it into words and use the words today?

Ex. **It is important to ask permission politely to borrow someone else's property because the more polite you are, the more likely they will be to let you use it.**

Ex. "May I use the blue crayon?"

"May I play with the blocks, too?"

"May I . . .

---

Suppose we had a day when five of us felt angry. What could we do to try to make it a good day?

Ex. **We could ask the five angry children to explain their feelings and see if there is some way to help them feel less angry.**

| We can | walk away | tap our toes ten times |
|---|---|---|
| | hum a tune | count to ten |
| | look at a book | etc. |

When someone gets angry with you, what are some ways that you can deal with their anger?

Ex.  **I can talk to the person in a quiet voice.**

**I can avoid getting angry myself.**

**I can count to ten.**

**I can try to calm the person by talking.**

**I can try to negotiate.**

---

What things make you angry?

Ex.  **I get angry when someone takes my belongings without asking me.**

**I get angry when someone pushes ahead of me in the line.**

**I get angry when someone cheats in a game.**

---

OK. So we feel mad. How can we "use our words" to tell about the anger rather than using our body?

Ex.  **We can say in a quiet voice what we think is wrong and what should be done to make it right. We should find a solution that pleases both sides.**

What is positive peer pressure?

**Positive peer pressure is being asked by friends or others to do something that is all right to do and that you may enjoy doing.**

Ex.  **. . . to play a game of baseball**

     **. . . to have dinner at their house**

     **. . . to go to the movies with them**

How do I react to positive peer pressure?

Ex.  **You may decide to do something if you are free and like doing it.**

     **You may say "No, thanks" if you have other more important or enjoyable things to do.**

     **You may simply say "Yes, I'd like to do that."**

What is negative peer pressure?

**Negative peer pressure is being asked by friends or others to do something that is wrong to do or something you do not like to do.**

Ex.  **. . . to make fun of another child**

     **. . . to steal something that belongs to someone else**

     **. . . to hurt an animal or another person**

How do I react to negative peer pressure?

Ex. **You may just say "NO!" in a nice way.**

**You may say, "Sorry, but I have other things to do."**

**You may tell them that you think it's the wrong thing to do and not for you.**

How do you feel about violence?

Ex. **I think violence is wrong because it hurts others and doesn't solve any problems.**

**I think violence only causes hatred and leads to more violence.**

**I think violence happens when people get too fearful and emotional and do not think before they act.**

How do you feel about non-violence?

Ex. **I think non-violence is the only way to settle arguments and solve problems between people.**

**I think non-violence is the only way to achieve real and lasting peace among people.**

# SOCIAL SKILLS TASK REVIEW Part II

*Directions:*   Display the following social skills related words on a colorful chart with a catchy title such as that used in the example on the following page.

Discuss one word with the children each day. Then review the words using a procedure such as one of these:

- Have children use a pointer, point to a word and explain what it means.

- Have a child point to a word and ask one of his/her classmates to tell what the word means.

- Give the meaning of a word and ask a child to point to the correct word.

| *Words* | *Sample Explanation* |
|---|---|
| Social Skills | what we need to get along with others |
| Conflict | a disagreement in ideas or interests |
| Attitude | how we think and act about someone or something |
| Compromise | an agreement in which each side gives up some demands or desires |
| Listening | to pay attention to what others are saying |
| Self-Image | how we think and feel about ourself and our abilities |
| Values | what we and others think are important and desirable to have |
| Peer Pressure | what our friends and peers want us to do |
| Negative Peer Pressure | what our peers want us to do but what is not right to do |
| Violence | fighting, shooting, hitting and more |
| Non-Violence | discussing, talking quietly, and more |

# SOMETHING TO QUACK ABOUT

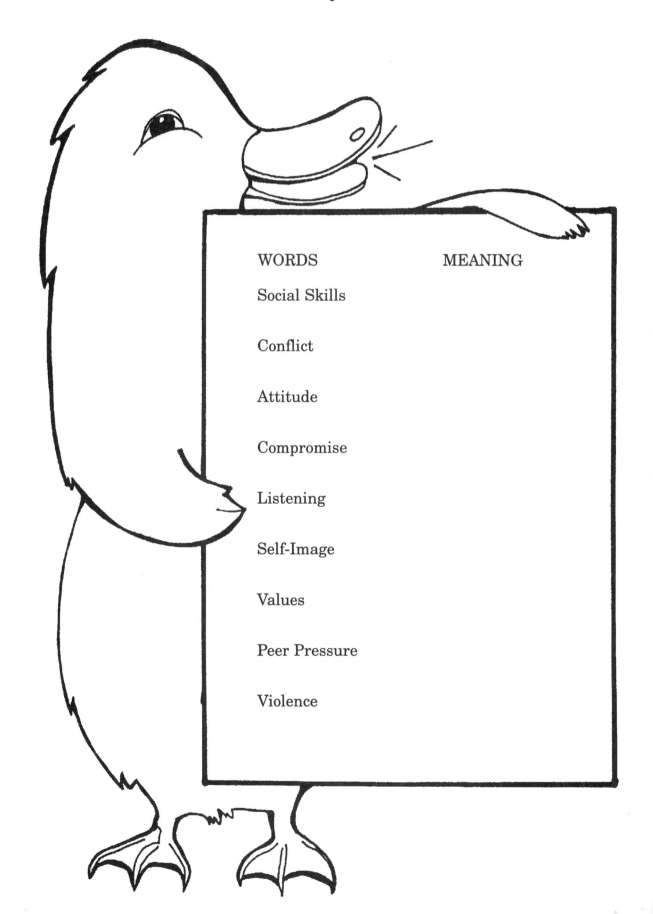

WORDS             MEANING

Social Skills

Conflict

Attitude

Compromise

Listening

Self-Image

Values

Peer Pressure

Violence

# SOCIAL SKILLS
# FAMILY TRAINING BOOKLET

The following pages present a social skills family training booklet entitled "Partners in Social Skills: A Family Affair" preceded by a "Family Letter" that introduces the booklet and can be signed by each child. The letter provides a good way to involve parents in the social skills development program to coordinate home and classroom instruction.

**NOTE: The letter and single plages of the booklet may be photocopied but only as many times as you need them for use with individual children, small groups, or an entire class. Reproduction of this material for an entire school system or for sale is strictly forbidden.**

You may order copies of the booklets from The Center for Applied Research in Education. The minimum quantity is twenty.

# FAMILY LETTER

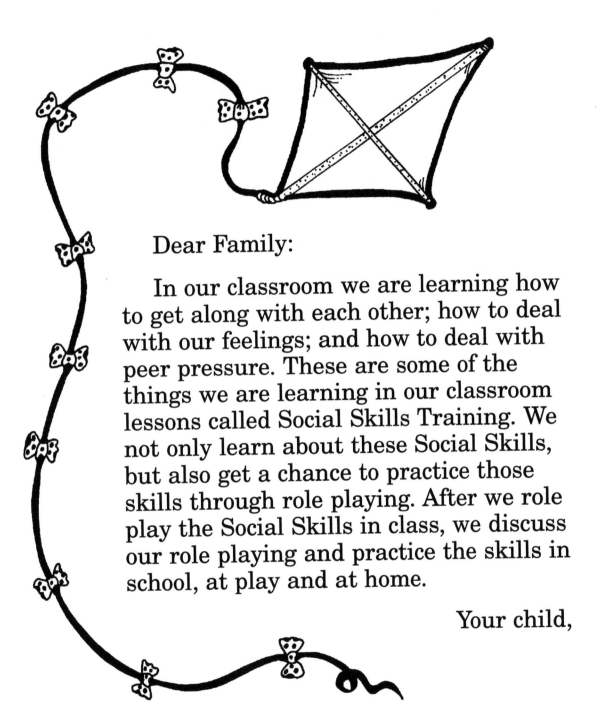

Dear Family:

In our classroom we are learning how to get along with each other; how to deal with our feelings; and how to deal with peer pressure. These are some of the things we are learning in our classroom lessons called Social Skills Training. We not only learn about these Social Skills, but also get a chance to practice those skills through role playing. After we role play the Social Skills in class, we discuss our role playing and practice the skills in school, at play and at home.

Your child,

## We are Flying High

# Partners
## in
## Social Skills

# A Family Affair

 **RUTH WELTMANN BEGUN, Editor**
The Society for Prevention of Violence
with
The Center for Applied Research in Education

## ACKNOWLEDGMENTS

The Founders, Trustees, Members, Friends of the Society for Prevention of Violence (SPV), and many Foundations and Corporations sponsored the writing of this social skills training booklet, "Partners in Social Skills: A Family Affair." The objective of the booklet is to acquaint the family with social skills training and how it can be used to resolve conflicts and to improve the behavior, attitude, and responsibility of the children and other family members. The booklet will help the family reinforce Social Skills Training being taught in schools and can also be used by the family to teach social skills to pre-school children.

Credit for writing the booklet belongs to a group of teachers from the Cleveland (Ohio) Public Schools who worked under the guidance of Ruth Weltmann Begun, then Executive Director of SPV. All participants utilized their expertise and considered many variations of instructional approaches and ideas until a format for the publication was agreed upon.

# INTRODUCTION

"Partners in Social Skills: A Family Affair" is a Social Skills Training resource guide to be used in a family setting. Social Skills Training helps a child to gain valuable skills such as self-esteem, self-control, respect for other persons, and responsibility for one's own actions. Such skills are very important for good family relationships, solid learning in school, and success all through life.

Some schools now offer Social Skills Training in their classrooms. For many children this supports what they are already learning at home. For many others, school is where they start to learn such skills. Many families today have single parents, or have two parents who both work, or have step-parents due to divorce and remarriage. All these changes put stress on families, and make parenting more challenging than in the past.

Today, the average child watches several hours of television each day, often without a parent or other adult present. TV scenes of violence or other harmful conduct can easily misguide young children.

This guide is designed to help parents in several ways:

(1) To introduce Social Skills Training to parents, and show them how this is already taught in some schools.

(2) To present some Social Skills Training activities that can be done at home.

(3) To encourage parents to apply this training with all of their children, even preschoolers.

(4) To remind parents that, no matter how much they may sometimes doubt it, *they* are the most important teachers in their children's lives.

The love, example, and guidance of parents and other adult family members can indeed make the difference for a child. He or she can learn, with their help, to respect others, make wise decisions, avoid violence, and become a successful and productive citizen as an adult.

Along the way, practicing the Social Skills included here should help the family enjoy a happier and less stressful home life.

THE SOCIAL SKILLS SONG
(Tune: "Mary Had a Little Lamb")

WE CAN USE OUR SOCIAL SKILLS
SOCIAL SKILLS, SOCIAL SKILLS
WE CAN USE OUR SOCIAL SKILLS
AS WE SPREAD OUR GOOD WILL

EVERY DAY IN EVERY WAY
EVERY WAY, EVERY WAY
EVERY DAY IN EVERY WAY
OUR CHARACTER WE BUILD

**S** elf-image improved
**O** nly giving compliments
**C** ompleting tasks
**I** gnoring distractions
**A** nger dealt with
**L** ess aggression

**S** eatwork and homework done
**K** eep following classroom rules
**I** gnoring teasing
**L** eave a troublesome situation
**L** earning to accept consequences
**S** taying out of fights

4

# TABLE OF CONTENTS

R = reproducible

1. Compliments
2. Asking Permission
3. Disciplinary Strategies
4. Respect for Others
5. Self-Respect
6. Improving Self-Image
7. Feelings
8. Accepting Consequences
9. Accepting Failure
10. Setting Goals
11. Dealing with Prejudice
12. Dealing with Anger
13. Peer Pressure
14. Problem Solving

# OUR FAMILY SOCIAL SKILLS TRAINING CHECKLIST

DIRECTIONS: Please fill out this checklist as a family before starting to read this book. Answer the way your family really feels by filling in the faces. There are no right or wrong answers.

This will help your family understand the need to practice Social Skills Training in your home.

| Almost Always | Sometimes | Almost Never |
|---|---|---|
| ☺ | 😐 | ☹ |

|  |  | Almost Always | Sometimes | Almost Never |
|---|---|---|---|---|
| 1. | Do we understand and follow when directions are given? | ☺ | 😐 | ☹ |
| 2. | Do we know and follow the rules in our home? | ☺ | 😐 | ☹ |
| 3. | Do we listen to adults in authority? | ☺ | 😐 | ☹ |
| 4. | Do we finish our household jobs? | ☺ | 😐 | ☹ |
| 5. | Do we take our finished homework to school the next day? | ☺ | 😐 | ☹ |
| 6. | Do we finish our housework even when others are not doing their share? | ☺ | 😐 | ☹ |
| 7. | Do we keep busy and quiet when waiting for our parent's attention? | ☺ | 😐 | ☹ |
| 8. | Do we find something quiet and helpful to do when we have free time? | ☺ | 😐 | ☹ |
| 9. | Do we deal with anger in a way that won't hurt others? | ☺ | 😐 | ☹ |
| 10. | Do we stay in control when somebody teases us? | ☺ | 😐 | ☹ |
| 11. | Do we think of ways other than fighting to handle our problems? | ☺ | 😐 | ☹ |
| 12. | Do we avoid fighting when someone threatens or hits us? | ☺ | 😐 | ☹ |
| 13. | Do we accept the consequences when we do something we shouldn't? | ☺ | 😐 | ☹ |
| 14. | Do we tell others that we like something nice about them or do something nice for them? | ☺ | 😐 | ☹ |
| 15. | Do we say and do nice things for ourselves when we have earned it? | ☺ | 😐 | ☹ |

# HELPFUL HINTS FOR USING THIS BOOK

1. Set aside quiet time and space.

2. Involve all family members.

3. Discussions should be friendly, positive and open.

4. Listen to each member's comments.

5. Criticism should be done in a positive and peaceful way.

6. All family members should work on being good role models.

# BE A ROLE MODEL FOR YOUR CHILD

- Let your child see you read. Visit the library with your child on a regular basis. At home, provide a quiet, well-lighted space for your child to study and read.

- Don't leave your children alone for long periods of time. Let your child know where and how to reach you. Leave your child with a happy feeling.

- Use kind and supportive words with your child. Unkind words can hurt as much as, or even more than, physical punishment.

- When resolving disputes or conflicts in the family, do your best to stay calm and in control of yourself.

- Beginning with yourself, make all family members responsible for keeping themselves and the house clean.

- Show your child how to "just say no" by your *own* saying no to drugs and other harmful activities.

- Remember that your child is learning from you, not only when you are telling him or her what to do, but *all* the time, by your example.

# Family Activity Page

Toot Your Own Horn

Write or draw five things you can
do well at home, at work, at school
or at play.

# FOURTEEN SELECTED SOCIAL SKILLS

The following pages contain fourteen selected Social Skills that have been taken from the "Social Skills Curriculum Activities Library" published by The Center for Applied Research in Education. Each skill is followed by skill activities. It is suggested that these activities can be done with all the family to develop the skill.

# FAMILY SOCIAL SKILLS

**Skill No. 1:**        **Giving Compliments:**

*Compliments mean saying something nice that makes someone else feel good.*

Do these skill activities with your family:

  1. Select someone to give a compliment.
  2. Think of a compliment that is pleasing and truthful.
  3. Say the compliment in a pleasant way.

**Skill No. 2:**        **Asking Permission:**

*Permission means giving consent.*

Do these skill activities with your family.

  1. Ask if you may borrow something.
  2. Do not take the item if the answer is no.
  3. If given permission, be careful with the item and return it in good condition.
  4. Say "thank you."

**Skill No. 3:**     **Disciplinary Strategies:**

*Discipline is training and conduct that develops self-control.*

Do these skill activities with your family:

1. Develop rules and consequences for family members.
2. Encourage all members to follow the rules.
3. Evaluate and change the rules when needed.

**Skill No. 4:**     **Respect for Others:**

*Respect means to be kind and courteous to others.*

Do these skill activities with your family:

1. Use the words "may I" when asking someone for something.
2. Use "please" and "thank you" when asking and receiving help.
3. Practice using these words often.

## Skill No. 5:        Using Self-Control:

*Self-control is remaining calm under stress and excitement.*

Do these skill activities with your family:

1. Stop and think about the situation that was causing stress to you and made you excited.
2. Count to ten while trying to remain calm.
3. Decide what you will do next.
4. Do it in a peaceful manner.


## Skill No. 6:        Improving Self-Image:

*Self-image is how you see yourself.*

Do these skill activities with your family:

1. Think of something you like about yourself.
2. Share it with your family members.
3. Discuss more ways you are special.


## Skill No. 7:        Expressing Feelings:

*Some feeling words are: happy, sad, angry, embarrassed, depressed, proud, guilty, frustrated and many more.*

Do these skill activities with your family:

1. Listen to the tone of voice, watch facial expressions and body gestures to understand the feelings in a message.
2. Ask the speaker if you understood his or her feelings correctly.

**Skill No. 8:**       **Accepting Consequences:**

*Accepting the results of one's own actions without complaining.*

Do these skill activities with your family:

    1. Decide if what you did was wrong.

    2. Admit what you did was wrong.

    3. Try to explain why you did it.

    4. Accept the punishment without complaint.


**Skill No. 9:**       **Reacting to Failure:**

*Failure is an unsuccessful attempt to achieve a goal.*

Do these skill activities with your family.

    1. Discuss what it means to fail.

    2. Decide why you failed.

    3. Accept the failure.

    4. Make a new plan to avoid making any similar mistakes.

## Skill No. 10: Setting Goals:

*Goals are plans of action which can be achieved.*

Do these skill activities with your family:

1. Think about things that need to be done at home or school.
2. Choose a goal and decide how it can be reached.
3. Reward yourself when you have reached your goal.


## Skill No. 11: Dealing with Prejudice:

*Prejudice is caused because of differences existing between people which are not acceptable to you.*

Do these skill activities with your family:

1. Discuss individual physical differences.
2. Discuss likenesses.
3. Treat everyone equally and with respect.
4. Discuss positive qualities and include everyone in your activities.


## Skill No. 12: Dealing with Anger:

*Everyone gets angry but anger must be resolved in a peaceful, verbal and non-physical manner.*

Do these skill activities with your family:

1. Stop and think about how you feel.
2. Think of non-threatening ways to handle your anger.
3. Choose an action that will resolve the conflict.
4. If there is no other choice, walk away.

**Skill No. 13:**      **Dealing with Peer Pressure:**

*Peer Pressure means that pressure is being strongly forced on you by friends, to do something you might or might not want to do. You might decide that what they want you to do is right or wrong.*

> We all have friends that we adore
> And that they like us we are sure
> We know they're friends because they care
> We know they're friends because they're fair
> Then there are others that are fakes
> We must watch out for our own sakes
> They'll try to get us to do much wrong
> So with these people we don't belong
> Say no to things you see are bad
> And for yourself you'll be glad
> Friends won't ask us to misbehave
> If you say no, we'll rave and rave.

After reading the poem do these skill activities with your family:

1. Decide if what your friends want you to do is right or wrong. If it seems wrong, consider the consequences. Don't join activities which hurt, damage others, or yourself. If caught you might be imprisoned and penalized. Say "NO" to drugs, alcohol and early sex. They will harm you.

2. Make a decision you can live with.

3. Think of other activities the group could participate in that are acceptable.

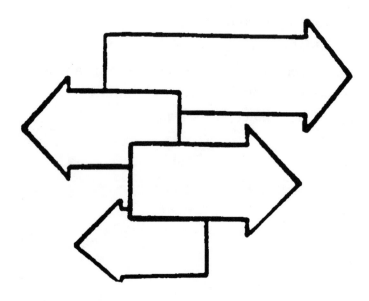

**Skill No. 14:**     **Problem Solving:**

*There are many ways to solve a problem and make a decision. All possibilities should be considered to find the best solution.*

Do these skill activities with your family:

    1. State the problem and list ways it can be solved.

    2. Select and try one of the choices.

    3. If it does not work try another solution until you find the best one.

# Family Activity Page

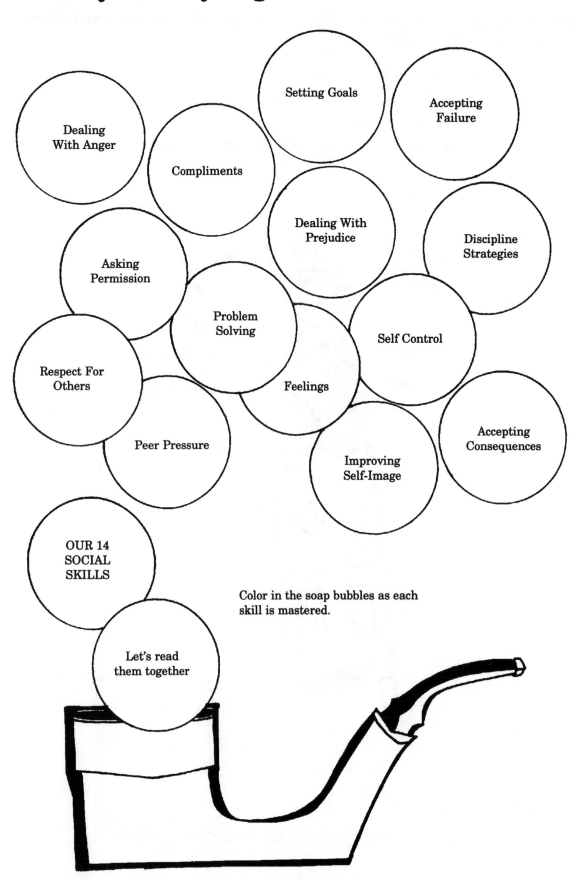

Setting Goals

Accepting Failure

Dealing With Anger

Compliments

Dealing With Prejudice

Discipline Strategies

Asking Permission

Problem Solving

Self Control

Respect For Others

Feelings

Peer Pressure

Accepting Consequences

Improving Self-Image

OUR 14 SOCIAL SKILLS

Color in the soap bubbles as each skill is mastered.

Let's read them together

# "MIRROR, MIRROR" POEM

Read the poem. Think of someone to compliment. Draw their picture, and write the compliment underneath.

Mirror, mirror on the wall
Give a compliment, and that's not all
Make it nice and make it kind
A deserving person is not hard to find.

# Family Activity Page, Certificate

Use this certificate to reward family members for proper use of social skills.

BEAR-R-Y GOOD FOR YOU!

NAME:

SKILLS:

DATE:

**Family Activity Page, Certificate**

# KEEP MOVING

# YOU ARE LOOKING GOOD!

**NAME:**

**SKILLS:**

**DATE:**

Use this certificate to reward family members for proper use of social skills.

# FAMILY TIME—GROUP DISCUSSIONS

**Directions to Family:** Please set aside ten to fifteen minutes daily to discuss the following questions with family members. During the family discussion be sure to listen to each other. Every family member should be encouraged to give input. Refer to the Social Skills listed in this book.

1. What Social Skills did you learn today?

2. What Social Skills did you use today?

3. What Social Skills did we use within our home?

4. What Social Skills did you use in solving a personal conflict?

5. Did you use courtesy words like "please" and "thank you" when requesting and receiving assistance?

6. What did you do today that made you feel proud?

7. What assignments including household chores did you complete today?

8. Were there any consequences that were difficult for you to accept?

9. How did you show respect for someone today?

10. Did you compliment someone today? How did this make you feel? How did this make the other person feel?

11. Which Social Skill will be our goal to work on tomorrow?

# WHAT MAKES YOU HAPPY?

***Directions to Family:*** It is suggested that all family members take part in this activity. Each member may list or draw three things that make them happy. (You may want to use additional paper.)

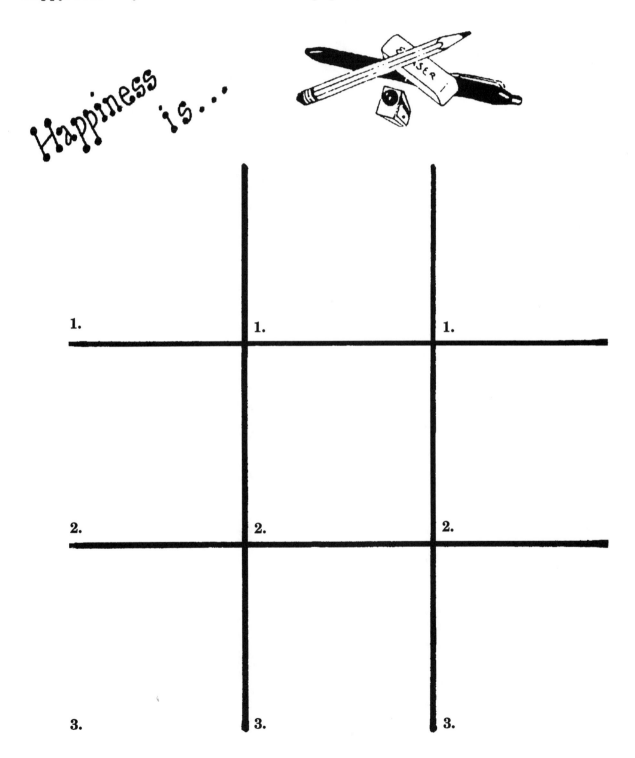

# PARENT-TEACHER COMMUNICATION

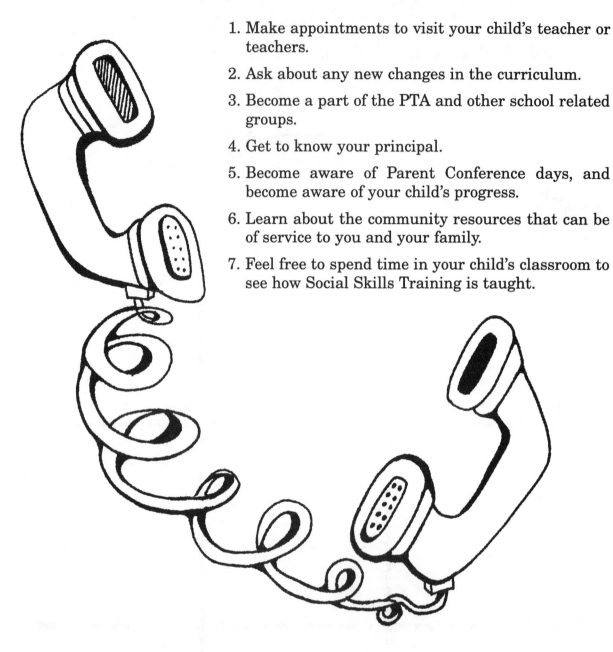

1. Make appointments to visit your child's teacher or teachers.

2. Ask about any new changes in the curriculum.

3. Become a part of the PTA and other school related groups.

4. Get to know your principal.

5. Become aware of Parent Conference days, and become aware of your child's progress.

6. Learn about the community resources that can be of service to you and your family.

7. Feel free to spend time in your child's classroom to see how Social Skills Training is taught.

After working on social skills, Mr. and Mrs. Mouse took their family on a cookout.

## Activity Color Page, Part II

Tommy Mouse and his sister were happy about the cookout. They watched their manners and talked about what fun they had making it a family affair. They all agreed to work, play, and respect one another. How about your family members?

# OUR FAMILY SOCIAL SKILLS TRAINING CHECKLIST

DIRECTIONS:     Please fill out this reaction sheet as a family, when you have completed this book.

This may be used to help your family better understand what Social Skills need to be reinforced within the home.

| Almost Always ☺ | Sometimes 😐 | Almost Never ☹ |
| --- | --- | --- |

| | | Almost Always | Sometimes | Almost Never |
| --- | --- | --- | --- | --- |
| 1. | Do we understand and follow when directions are given? | ☺ | 😐 | ☹ |
| 2. | Do we know and follow the rules in our home? | ☺ | 😐 | ☹ |
| 3. | Do we listen to adults in authority? | ☺ | 😐 | ☹ |
| 4. | Do we finish our household jobs? | ☺ | 😐 | ☹ |
| 5. | Do we take our finished homework to school the next day? | ☺ | 😐 | ☹ |
| 6. | Do we finish our housework even when others are not doing their share? | ☺ | 😐 | ☹ |
| 7. | Do we keep busy and quiet when waiting for our parent's attention? | ☺ | 😐 | ☹ |
| 8. | Do we find something quiet and helpful to do when we have free time? | ☺ | 😐 | ☹ |
| 9. | Do we deal with anger in a way that won't hurt others? | ☺ | 😐 | ☹ |
| 10. | Do we stay in control when somebody teases us? | ☺ | 😐 | ☹ |
| 11. | Do we think of ways other than fighting to handle our problems? | ☺ | 😐 | ☹ |
| 12. | Do we avoid fighting when someone threatens or hits us? | ☺ | 😐 | ☹ |
| 13. | Do we accept the consequences when we do something we shouldn't? | ☺ | 😐 | ☹ |
| 14. | Do we tell others that we like something nice about them or do something nice for them? | ☺ | 😐 | ☹ |
| 15. | Do we say and do nice things for ourselves when we have earned it? | ☺ | 😐 | ☹ |

© 1995 by Society for Prevention of Violence

27

# GUIDELINES FOR CARING PARENTS

I.  How your children learn to act depends on what they are taught—and YOU are their most important teacher.

II.  Your children will learn more from watching what you do than from listening to what you say to do.

III.  Remember that you were once a child, and treat your children with patience and understanding.

IV.  Be fair, be consistent, and respect your children as you would have them respect you.

V.  Stay close to your children, but give them room to learn from their own experiences and to think for themselves.

VI.  Show your children things in life that are beautiful, and show that you appreciate these things.

VII.  Love your children with all your heart, your mind and your strength, and everything else will follow.

Dedicated to all family members who accept the challenge of helping each other develop into mature, healthy, stable, responsible and productive citizens.

29